"A brilliant tour de force. To put market share ahead of profit is 'fool's gold,' as Miniter suggests. His story of Mr. Rustici, a small retailer who profited from below-cost market share strategy by Wal-Mart, is alone worth the price of the book (found in chapter one). This book is must reading for all CEOs and corporate strategists."

> —Mark Skousen, president, Foundation for
> Economic Education

"Every business leader, investor, and entrepreneur needs to read contrarian thinkers. Richard Miniter writes in that valuable tradition. This book presents some uncomfortable truths about market share and the intriguing business success of those managers who ignore it."

> —Michael Useem, Professor of Management and
> Director of the Center for Leadership and
> Change Management at the Wharton School,
> University of Pennsylvania

"If Bernie Ebbers, Jean-Marie Messier, Ken Lay, and their fellow CEOs had read *The Myth of Market Share,* they might still have jobs—and market share, too. But it's not too late for you: Read Richard Miniter's book, profit by it (literally), and savor a refreshing blast of real iconoclasm."

> —Andrew Ferguson, columnist, *Bloomberg News*

"Business journalists tend to repeat each other like out-of-tune choirboys. Miniter jumps off the bandwagon and raises the kind of contrarian questions that business leaders or anyone interested in understanding the political economy need to think hard about."

"A readable, entertaining call for business leaders to check their egos at the door, temper their quest for size, and return to common sense and basic values of free enterprise. It's about profit, not publicity. It's about cash flow, not size or market share."

"The experience of America as compared to Japan shows that the market share theory was always insane. Miniter does even more to explode the myth of market share by demonstrating ways in which midsized firms can beat their larger rivals."

"In 192 pithy pages, Richard Miniter attacks the ever-hip if century-old management idea that increasing market share is the absolute key to a company's growth and ultimate profits. The collapse of the dot.com-, telecommunications-, internet-bubble threw market share mania onto its deathbed. In *The Myth of Market Share,* Miniter drives a lively, well-argued stake through its heart."

"Miniter's book is sure to shake up the conventional thinking about market share and profits. Let it come down!"
—Sam Dealey, editor, *The International Economy*

"Economists know why pursuing market share will usually hurt a firm's profits. With solid reasoning and great stories, *The Myth of Market Share* will give you that same understanding."
—David R. Henderson, Research Fellow, Hoover Institution, and author of *The Joy of Freedom: An Economist's Odyssey*

"Too many businesses have big misconceptions. They're too busy chasing mergers and market share instead of pursuing their long-term health and wealth. Miniter's book is the antidote."
—Stephen Pollard, Senior Fellow, Civitas (London)

"As manager of one of Europe's largest insurance investment funds and as dean of one of Europe's leading business schools, I caution my students and my analysts not to forget the fundamentals. Now I can tell them, 'Just read Richard Miniter's *The Myth of Market Share*.'"
—Eric Briys, CEO and chairman, Cyberlibris, and coauthor of *The Fisherman and the Rhinoceros*

"Richard Miniter's *The Myth of Market Share* is made-to-order for Asia's aspiring corporate leaders. It offers a recipe for success in the increasingly competitive global market."

—Brett M. Decker, *The Asian Wall Street Journal*

"Miniter's book reveals for the first time that the concept of market share was created by the critics of business. Here is a better vision of a global economy with the energy of a truly free and profit-driven marketplace."

—Johan Norberg, author of *In Defense of Global Capitalism*

"As a seasoned investigative journalist, Miniter challenges conventional business wisdom with such energy and humor."

—Stephen Grey, *The Sunday Times* (London)

"Richard Miniter, in this closely argued and well-researched book, is all too convincing about the follies of chasing market share and neglecting profits. Such a strategy is indeed fool's gold and, moreover, always has been."

—Ruth Lea, The Institute for Directors (London)

"Miniter spares no sacred cows in *The Myth of Market Share*. He goes right to what works, what doesn't, and why."

—Tom Switzer, *The Australian* (Australia's largest daily)

THE MYTH OF
MARKET SHARE

THE MYTH OF
MARKET SHARE

WHY MARKET SHARE IS
THE FOOL'S GOLD OF BUSINESS

RICHARD MINITER

CROWN
BUSINESS
NEW YORK

Published by Crown Business, New York, New York.
Member of the Crown Publishing Group, a division of Random House, Inc.

www.randomhouse.com

CROWN BUSINESS is a trademark and the Rising Sun colophon is a registered trademark of Random House, Inc.

Printed in the United States of America

Design by Meryl Sussman Levavi/Digitext

Library of Congress Cataloging-in-Publication Data
Miniter, Richard.
    The myth of market share: why market share is the fool's gold of business / Richard Miniter.—1st ed.
    Includes bibliographical references.
    1. Market share. I. Title.
    HD2757.15.M56   2002
    658.4'012—dc21 2002004807

ISBN 0-609-60988-2

10 9 8 7 6 5 4 3 2 1

First Edition

To Leola Tobin, who always believed,
and Janie Kong, for everything

DILBERT

Contents

Introduction

The young tycoon-to-be leaned closer to tell me his secret. It was 1998 and he had asked me to join him in the library of a private club in Washington, D.C., to tell me about his business plan. His Alexandria, Virginia–based software firm was about to take off, he said. Then he told me his secret: "Build market share."

Market share? That's right. Once the company became the largest seller in its category, it would be able to charge a fortune for its services. It is not like the old economy, he assured me. "But market share is key. Everything depends on that."

At the time, thousands of conversations like that were going on all over the world. Now, most of those dot-coms have become dot-bombs. They burned up their venture capital and faded away like shooting stars. Many observers have clucked their tongues and chalked up the whole dot-com boom to "irrational exuberance" or youthful hubris. Pride goeth before the fall and all that.

But managers, investors, and entrepreneurs have overlooked a more important lesson. *Many so-called old economy companies are pursuing the same market-share strategies.* They have actual earnings, so they are not about to disappear anytime soon. But they are hobbling themselves with an outmoded strategy that didn't work for the robber barons and definitely won't work in today's hyperlinked, globalized economy. Now, more than ever, corporations need a sensible strategy for sustainable profits—not a faddish formula from consultants.

This conversation got me thinking. As a longtime contributor to the *Wall Street Journal*'s "Manager's Journal" column and, later, as the *Wall Street Journal Europe*'s editor of its weekly "Business Europe" column, it was my job to stay a step ahead of business trends. So I began to investigate the connection between market share and profits.

The more I examined business plans built on chasing market share, the more I saw the same strategy employed in many different lines of business. It seemed as if nearly everyone was acting like a dot-com, chasing market share and saying that profits would come later. Customers were forgotten as competitors measured themselves against one another. Costs were shrugged off as visions bloomed.

Pets.com was typical. Its first annual report announced that the company expected to lose money until it had garnered the dominant market share in the online pet-product category. It was one of the purest examples of the transcendental belief in market share. Pets.com has since gone under.

Yet the venerable giant AT&T has virtually the same strategy. Each month the phone giant mails out millions of checks that can be cashed only when the recipient agrees to switch long-distance service—literally buying market share. Of course, MCIWorldCom and Sprint do the same thing. Some savvy customers now switch only long enough to cash the check or to play the long-distance giants off against one another, often bidding up the bribe to $100. There are no reliable estimates of how much this costs the phone giants, but the motivation is no mystery—market share. Through it all, market-share ratios among the top three firms have remained virtually the same—while the profit margins in the long-distance business have been slowly seeping away.

When Sprint slashed its nighttime long-distance rate to five cents per minute in the summer of 1999, MCI soon matched it. By August, AT&T admitted to analysts that it was losing sales and market share. AT&T responded by reducing long-distance rates to seven cents per minute all day, seven days per week, for an additional $5.95 monthly fee. On the day that AT&T unveiled its market-share-preserving strategy, its stock dropped 4.7 percent.

This book starts with a very simple question: Does market-share growth lead to long-term growth in profits? One answer to the question—yes, more share is better—is considered blindingly obvious to legions of executives, consultants, and business school professors. But it is based on blind faith. The more one looks for evidence, the harder it is to sustain a belief in a market-share strategy.

In the end, managers must choose between two rival schools of thought: market leadership or profit leadership. A business can have only one focus and a manager can choose only one alternative.

One strategy is market leadership: to seize a commanding share of the market and wield that elusive Excalibur, pricing power. Managers following this philosophy are often blindly following the outmoded strategies that they learned in their business school days. Or they are captives of internal and external constituencies—everyone from the union boss and the regional vice president defending his unprofitable plants to the journalists and analysts who keep asking: "Why didn't you grow your share last quarter?"

The alternative philosophy may sound basic and uncomplicated, but it works. It's called profit leadership. Profit leaders think about customers, not competitors, and think about next quarter's opportunities, not justifying last quarter's market share.

In this book, I show that the market-share theory flatly doesn't work in most industries most of the time. I examine every significant argument for chasing market share and show that, in the real world, the "advantages" of market share don't add up to much. And I provide a blueprint for companies to transform themselves into profit leaders.

When I began my investigation into the strange relationship between market share and profitability, I set a few ground rules. *First, I would focus on results, not theories or promises.* Corporate strategies would be evaluated just as any sensible investor evaluates them, by seeing if the strategy yields a higher return on investment than all its reasonable alternatives.

Second, I started with the view *that companies exist solely to make profits for their owners, the shareholders;* and managers are supposed to pursue policies designed to maximize long-term shareholder value. Of course, that is much easier said than done. That is why evidence, not opinion or belief, is crucial.

Third, I acknowledged that *managers must make hard decisions in a rapidly changing marketplace.* The only fair way to measure the quality of those decisions is to compare those decisions against those of their direct competitors, not some theoretical ideal or some hypothetical best case. More often than not, firms with smaller market shares seemed to be earning better margins. So companies, throughout this book, are compared against their rivals in terms of return on capital invested and similar measures.

Fourth, in this analysis, *there will be very little patience for so-called long-term strategies that fail to deliver within a few years.* This is not short-term thinking. The fundamentals of the marketplace are evolving very rapidly, product cycles are shortening, new sales channels are emerging, and new competitive threats can appear suddenly. If a company does not see results on its investment within a few years, chances are that the rationale for those investments will disappear before the results appear. This is often the case with managers who argue that a company needs to make a large, up-front investment in a larger market share that will supposedly pay dividends down the road. When those investments yield results, they will be praised. When they do not—and they mostly do not—they will be pilloried.

Fifth, it is important to remember that *every rule has a sensible exception.* I do not shy away from the evidence that shows that in certain industries, at certain times, a strategy based on market share is the best approach for long-term growth and above-average returns on investment. (We will take a closer look at those exceptions in Chapter Six.)

Finally, there is one up-front question that I make no attempt to dodge: *Why do some enterprises, with the largest market shares, seem to earn the highest returns in their industry?* This is especially clear in the shoe manufacturing business, in pet-food sales, and in much of what General Electric Co. does. What sets these firms apart is that they treat market share not as a goal, but as a benchmark for their constant efforts at improvement.

The last point is subtle, but critical. Many companies say that market share is just a tool for evaluating their efforts, but, in fact, their managers see it as a goal. They aim to achieve or maintain a certain share of the market. What sets very profitable large firms apart from their competitors is that *these firms treat market share as a byproduct.* These profit leaders, as I explain in Chapter Five, have other goals. Their internal and external incentives are arranged not to reward market-share targets, but the stated goals of the company. Market share is simply a tool—one among many. It isn't what the company is about—although many of those firms have the largest share in their industry.

Some companies are already moving away from market share as a strategic focus. But as poet T. S. Eliot notes, the greatest treason is to do the right thing for the wrong reason.

Managers need to know why they are making certain strategic decisions and not others.

The go-go stock market is gone. The venture capitalists now want to see solid profits, not promising projections. There is no more free money floating around—it is high time to put profit back at the center of business.

Still, many companies and industry sectors—take the European mobile-phone sector—are still partying like it's 1999. They are burning capital to buy market share.

Let me be clear. I am not saying that companies should ignore market share, although it would probably not hurt them if they did. Market share should simply be seen as a by-product, a secondary effect, of pursuing a company's core mission. Market share is not an advantage, by itself. It is *the result* of a sustainable competitive advantage, not the *cause*.

If investors and managers are ever going to benefit from the painful education taught by the slowing economy, they will have to learn the lessons of market share and profits. Those who refuse to learn will only pay their tuition in the form of lost profits, diminished opportunities, and lackluster growth. If you decide to convert away from the false god of market share, this book is full of examples of enterprises that moved from worshiping size to honoring profit.

THE MYTH OF
MARKET SHARE

CHAPTER ONE

Fool's Gold: Why the Myth of Market Share Is Wrecking the World's Great Companies

IN READING THE HISTORY OF NATIONS, WE FIND
THAT, LIKE INDIVIDUALS, THEY HAVE THEIR WHIMS
AND THEIR PECULIARITIES; THEIR SEASONS OF EX-
CITEMENT AND RECKLESSNESS, WHEN THEY CARE
NOT WHAT THEY DO. WE FIND THAT WHOLE COMMUNI-
TIES SUDDENLY FIX THEIR MINDS UPON ONE OBJECT,
AND GO MAD IN ITS PURSUIT; THAT MILLIONS OF
PEOPLE BECOME SIMULTANEOUSLY IMPRESSED WITH
ONE DELUSION, AND RUN AFTER IT . . .

—*MEMOIRS OF EXTRAORDINARY POPULAR DELUSIONS*
CHARLES MACKAY (1841)

THE OBSESSION

Business leaders are gripped by the cult of size, the dogma of bigness.

They are mad for market share. Nearly every company is mesmerized by it. Keeping it, growing it, justifying it—

try to talk to a senior executive without the subject coming up. "I can't predict the economy," Scott McNealey, the legendary chief executive of Sun Microsystems, told *Barron's* recently, "but we will gain share."

Nearly every time I meet with a CEO or senior executive, market share comes up. The reason is no mystery: Top executives know that they are measured by it, and they know that they measure their subordinates by it.

Market share is also an obsession among Wall Street analysts, institutional investors, financial journalists, growth-minded entrepreneurs, high-flying consultants, self-styled gurus, and almost everyone with a 401(k). It seems like a neat shorthand for understanding the value and growth potential of any stock or business plan. It is easy, deceptively easy—and, too often, wrong.

Why do so many people believe that market share naturally and inevitably leads to world-beating profits?

Most business schools are temples to market share and churn out more acolytes every year. The guy in the big corner office is always asking about it. On the conference call, the fund manager wants to know why share isn't growing. The consultants always seem to have a magic plan to produce more market share. And when was the last time you heard someone say that his business plan would succeed in *reducing* market share?

Like all dogmatic beliefs, followers explain away all of the contrary evidence or simply ignore what they cannot explain.

Periodically, a researcher will emerge with new evidence about market share and profits. Eyes weary from poring over earnings reports, the unwelcome prophet will say something like: "Market share is the fool's gold of business. It looks valuable and it takes a lot of hard work to get—but it is nearly worthless. It wastes time and money while the competition is digging out the real thing. It hobbles, cripples, and kills great companies!" And, like most prophets, he will be ignored.

Maybe the discouraged prophet will drop his yellow legal-size tablets on the ground, allowing us to read his notes: "The market-share obsession, based on flawed and outmoded theories, drags down corporate profits and pushes companies into costly moves. It makes companies bigger without making them more profitable." Sometimes it seems to coincide with profits; too often it does not.

This book is about two powerful ideas: the obsession of market share and the proven path to profits. Once decision makers understand the misguided role that market share plays in corporate strategy, this book will show them how some companies achieve strong growth and above-average profits, using techniques that have worked in a broad array of industries.

It will not make the true believers happy.

THE CULT OF SIZE

Let's start by looking into the world that really matters—the realm of results.

Consider the roll call of companies that achieved large shares of the market in their industry sector or dominated their line of business. Far from being dominant giants, many were sold, were acquired in hostile takeovers, or simply went bankrupt. And the rest? They remain ailing giants—respected behemoths whose executives mumble that Wall Street analysts don't understand their business or claim their sector is having a "cyclical downturn." Still others say they are just one more restructuring effort away from the golden age of profits and market dominance. Sure.

The following companies—in vastly different sectors—have only two things in common: They focused on market share and failed to earn as much money as their competitors.

- Amazon.com is a Brobdingnagian straight out of Jonathan Swift's *Gulliver's Travels,* which it probably sells more of than any other bookstore in the world. It is easily the nation's largest online book purveyor and moves more volumes than almost all of its bricks-and-mortar rivals. One small problem: Despite seven years of market-share growth, it didn't report a net profit until January 2002. The profit was tiny: $5 million on $1.12 billion in sales. Even that slim profit would have disappeared if the euro hadn't declined against the dollar, slashing some $16 million worth of its euro-denominated debt.

- DEC once had a large share of the minicomputer business. But profits slipped, as market share remained firm. DEC was rescued by Compaq. Now Compaq itself is in trouble. But Compaq's CEO, Michael Capellas, told *Fortune* magazine that he will not make DEC's mistakes; "We will cede market share to protect profits." Mr. Capellas must have learned something since March 1996 when he stated that he would sacrifice profit to build market share. But, in the end, Compaq couldn't transform itself into a profit-centered company. Old habits die hard. By 2001, Compaq was desperate to be acquired by Hewlett-Packard, a merger effort that soon led to a nasty proxy battle.

Even today's most successful companies could be more profitable if they cared less about market share.

- Wal-Mart, founded by the legendary Sam Walton, is hugely profitable. But, as a case study later in this chapter reveals, the company is focused on expanding into new markets—whether they are fully profitable or not. As a result, Wal-Mart is less profitable than its two smaller competitors, Family Dollar and Dollar General, from which investors earned more on a rate-of-return basis.

- 3M, the maker of Scotch tape and Post-it notes, is gargantuan, a $15 billion business that towers over its competitors in nearly every product category. At least in size. Yet others earn more profit in many categories. "3M is a $25 billion business trapped inside a happy, fat $15 billion company," one consultant, who has worked with 3M for more than a decade, told me. 3M is too busy running after tomorrow's products to catch today's profits, too busy innovating to focus on selling and serving its customers. Less innovative rivals quickly move in, snatching sales that should have been 3M's. Innovation is good, but failing to fully exploit the profit potential of its new products in the name of market share hasn't helped 3M become the next GE.

IS BIGGER BETTER?

The more that one looks for evidence of big companies exploiting their market share and superior scale to earn outsize returns, the more one finds evidence to the contrary.

It appears that larger market share, by itself, doesn't equal larger profits. Although some companies have succeeded in exploiting the benefits of size, most have only become bigger.

Take the American banking sector. The biggest originator of home mortgages in the first half of 2000 was Chase Manhattan Mortgage. Was it the most profitable on a net earnings basis? Not by a long shot. The most profitable was Washington Mutual, the number five ranked lender, which earned $452 million. By contrast, Chase Manhattan Mortgage earned less than $123 million.[1]

Why didn't Chase Manhattan do better?

Bankers are fond of saying that the cost of servicing a $100,000 mortgage is equal to the cost of servicing a $200,000 mortgage. All other things equal, the bank that has the highest average loan size is the most profitable.

Chase's problem was its low average loan size: $120,000. In terms of average loan size, Chase ranked thirty-ninth nationwide. To generate high volume, it had to take on many smaller, relatively less profitable loans. So Chase was bringing in more volume, but with a lower return. Why build volume instead of profiting like Washington Mutual? Market-share madness is the most likely culprit.

Indeed, market-share madness seems to grip every industry—and analysts and investors are starting to notice. When three European steel companies announced a three-way merger to form the world's largest steelmaker, I phoned a London-based Commerzbank steel industry analyst, Peter Dupont. He immediately summed up the foolish fascination with market share in that industry: "A touching sign of faith for the cult of size."

ARTICLES OF FAITH

Market share is treated like an article of religious faith, unquestioned and unquestionable. Virtually every study on market share—and over the last forty years a small mountain of market-share studies has been published on both sides of the Atlantic—simply assumes a direct connection between market-share growth and profitability. Here is an old, but classic, example: "Capturing a dominant share of a market is likely to mean enjoying the highest profits of any companies serving that market," Paul Bloom and Philip Kotler once wrote in a 1975 *Harvard Business Review* article.

That sentiment appeared over and over again in dozens of major business journal articles in the past few decades and it was often the unstated assumption in hundreds more. Those studies became part of the curricula at business schools around the world and worked their way into the popular business press—everything from *Harvard Business Review* and the *Wall Street Journal* to *Fortune* and *Business 2.0.* Over the years, managers decided to listen to the "experts"—and those studies became the bricks in the foundation of thousands of business plans and corporate strategies. Soon nearly everyone believed that market-share growth meant higher profits. Few bothered to actually look at what the research showed about the tenuous link between market share and profits.

Even powerful dissenters were ignored. One of the giants of American economics, Harold Demsetz, a professor emeritus at the University of California at Los Angeles, noted: "Alternative explanations for this data generally were ignored because the market concentration doctrine had won the imagination of investigators and given direction to their thoughts, much as Ptolemaic astronomy [the idea that the sun revolved around the earth] provided the signposts for the study of heavenly bodies the four hundred years surrounding the life of Christ."[2] In other words, researchers saw what they wanted to see.

But what about the evidence to the contrary? What about the studies that tested the assumed correlation between market share and higher than average returns and found the dogma lacking? In 1982, Carolyn Y. Woo, a professor at Purdue University's Graduate School of Management, and Purdue professor Arnold C. Cooper published a powerful article in the *Harvard Business Review*. It was called "The Surprising Case for Low Market Share." It detailed a number of companies that earned much higher returns than their much-larger competitors. Their conclusion challenged the conventional wisdom with a wealth of evidence: "Low market share does not inevitably lead to low profitability. Despite the well-accepted correlation between market share and profitability, market share is not a necessary condition for profitability." But Ms. Woo and Mr. Cooper were challenging the consultant catechism, and the "cult of size" kept most of its believers.

Other researchers pointed out that the much-touted correlation between market share and profitability was in fact mistaking cause for effect. One study warned against accepting the idea that market share and profitability were linked.[3] Instead both are dependent on product quality, price, costs, distribution, marketing, resources, strategic objectives, and so on. Market share, rather than leading to profitability, was the *result* of successful business practices that also led to profitability. Profits may be the result of "unobservable factors such as managerial skill and luck. . . . That is, market share may not strictly cause business success but rather be a consequence/outcome of it," noted another study.[4] But these voices in the wilderness were soon forgotten. The conventional wisdom remained impervious to contrary evidence. Consultants had advice to sell, executives had plans to justify, and entrepreneurs had dreams to chase.

Market-share madness marched on without missing a step. Why? Perhaps these studies simply made too many consultants and executives uncomfortable. How can you question what everyone "knows"?

The most thorough student of market share and profitability I've talked to is Donald V. Potter, president of Windermere Associates, a Moraga, California–based consulting firm. A veteran of Andersen Consulting with more than thirty years of experience in a range of businesses, Mr. Potter is an affable Californian with an easy manner, but also a former U.S. Marine with a tenacious will. He, too, compares belief in the power of market share to pure faith. "It is like trying to change someone's religion," he told me.

He and his team examined more than 3,000 public companies in 240 industries. Mr. Potter's results shatter the conventional wisdom on market share and profits. He discovered that more than 70 percent of the time *the firm with the biggest share of the market doesn't have the highest rate of return.*

The 1997 Windermere study examined some 240 industries that have at least five competitors whose individual annual sales are each greater than $50 million. Among the top four firms in each of 240 industries, the

market-share leader led the industry in pretax returns on
assets only 29 percent of the time—only 4 percent better
than random chance. Barely beating random chance
doesn't seem like much of a benefit for a corporate strategy that costs tens of millions of dollars in management
time and consulting fees—but that is the best the market-
share strategy can deliver on average.

And, chances are, the lucky 29 percent—who lead
their industry in both size and profits—are doing something very different from their less successful peers in
other industries. (We will find out what sets these companies apart in Chapter Five.)

Now let's look at the other end of the spectrum: the
firms in the number four position, the ones with the
smallest market share among the top four in each line of
business studied. Twenty-three percent of the time, these
firms had *higher* returns than each of their three larger
rivals did. If market share were an essential ingredient to
above-average profitability, these relatively small fry
should not even have been contenders. Instead, almost one
out of every four times, they were the most profitable.
Clearly market share alone doesn't seem that closely connected to profits.

Some might think their industry is special—that in
their case, market share is essential. Highly concentrated,
capital-intensive enterprises—everything from petroleum
refineries to food processing conglomerates—need scale
and market share to be competitive, or so goes the theory.
Again, the Windermere research and the evidence do not
support this view. In highly concentrated industries, market
leaders did only slightly better than average. They had the
best industry returns only 38 percent of the time, according
to the Windermere study. If market share alone were the

key to success in these industries, wouldn't the biggest enterprise be the most profitable much more than one-third of the time? Remember, in highly concentrated sectors, there are usually only a handful of real contenders. Dumb luck may prove to be a better predictor of outsize profits in highly concentrated businesses—not market share.

Others say that high-growth sectors require market-share strategies. But, again, the facts tell a different story. High-growth industries actually did slightly worse than average, according to the Windermere study. Only 27 percent of high-market-share businesses in high-growth sectors had the best industry rate of return—compared with the average of 29 percent for all industries.

Though the Windermere study tracked profits in terms of return on assets, the results would be virtually identical if profits were measured in terms of return on equity, says Mr. Potter.

The bottom line seems inescapable—size doesn't automatically lead to profits. After all, firms with big shares of the market usually underperform their peers while relatively smaller firms are about as likely to prosper.

Case Study: International Paper Co.

This is a lesson that International Paper Co. seems to be learning the hard way. If growing market share were the path to riches and glory, then International Paper Co. CEO John T. Dillon would be a happy man. His company is the world's largest paper producer. So far, he is far from happy.

For years the paper maker faced a boom-and-bust cycle. When paper demand climbed, paper companies would flood the market with paper—often opening new plants to pump up the volume. Then supply would swell, prices would collapse, and the paper industry would gasp for air. Some would fail; others would be sold. Then the survivors would start the cycle again.

Mr. Dillon vowed to break the grip of boom-bust—by increasing market share. His motivation couldn't be clearer. After an interview with Mr. Dillon, here's how *BusinessWeek* described the strategy: "The way out of these lackluster results is to get bigger. With size comes greater market share and, it is hoped, some control over IP's prices."[5]

With this strategy in mind, International Paper has been on a buying spree. Federal Paperboard was snapped up for $3.8 billion in March 1996. Then IP bought one of the largest makers of office printer and copier paper, Union Camp, for some $7.1 billion in April 1999. Next, it acquired Champion Paper Corp. for $9.6 billion in June 2000. Total sales topped $28 billion in 2000—making IP bigger than some industries and the largest in its own.

But size didn't translate into profits. Return on invested capital is roughly 7 percent—still significantly below that of rival paper makers, which are much smaller. Let's not lose sight of that return on capital figure—investors could easily earn a much better return in a run-of-the-mill mutual fund. And IP executives know that investors are starting to unfavorably compare the company's stock to savings accounts. Returns to shareholders are "simply unacceptable," John Faraci, the company's chief financial officer, told shareholders in May 2001. In August, Faraci admitted to *Barron's* that IP "experienced only one year in the past decade in which returns exceeded the company's cost of capital."

International Paper's stock has actually dropped in value over the last five years. Meanwhile, all of those acquisitions have left behind a debt hangover of some $15.5 billion—roughly four times annual cash flow.

What about pricing power—surely all those acquisitions gave the company some ability to control prices? Not so far. Take a look at the magazine paper market, usually a very profitable niche. When IP bought Champion, it combined two large slices of the magazine paper market. It now holds a commanding share of the market—but prices are falling. Magazine publishers are demanding steep discounts, and the giant paper maker is giving them. By the end of 2001, IP was blaming the business cycle, the slowing economy, and the September 11 terrorist attacks for its weak performance. Everything but its misguided market-share strategy.

What went wrong? Part of the problem is that low-cost producers in Southeast Asia and Brazil can rush in whenever International Paper tries to close down U.S. plants and raise prices. And, short of 100 percent market share worldwide or high tariffs, International Paper simply can't shut them out. On the high end, Swedish and Finnish producers have higher productivity. No amount of market-share growth is going to change that, either.

The only market that matters is the world market—and no company can ever become big enough to beat the entire world. Increasing globalization will only underline this fact.

SECONDARY EFFECTS

The International Paper case tells us something else, too: that the pursuit of market share can lead companies to make a series of questionable moves, in the hopes of boosting share. In this case, it was a string of costly, ill-fated acquisitions.

But pursuit of market share, once market share is made the centerpiece of corporate strategy, can lead to other questionable moves. Executives and managers often find themselves "forced" to make a series of risky decisions—deep discounts, cheap financing, and unprofitable or thinly profitable sales—just to defend or boost market share. These actions reduce profit margins, erode brand identity, and harm the long-term health of companies. As long as companies spend on the market-share treadmill, profits seem farther and farther away. (We will treat this problem in greater detail in Chapter Four.)

And a market-share strategy comes with risks. Obsessive focus on market share can undermine the relationship between a company's intellectual property—including its brand, its image, its intangible worth to the public—and its customers and shareholders.

Case Study: Izod Lacoste and the "Anemic Alligator"

Consider the cautionary tale of the Izod Lacoste polo shirt. Rene Lacoste, a 1930s French tennis champion, created the legendary shirt. His distinctive crocodile emblem soon developed real cachet, fetching high prices and earning fat margins. The brand really took off after President Eisenhower was spotted wearing the trademark alligator and a gaggle of golf-playing celebrities soon followed.

In the 1970s Lacoste sold the U.S. rights to its polo shirt and alligator emblem to General Mills, a Minneapolis-based conglomerate. Sticking to the high-price, high-margin strategy, General Mills had, by 1980, turned

Lacoste shirts into a $400 million business in the United States. It peaked at $450 million in 1982.

Then the company began discounting to increase market share. Sales fell, triggering another round of price cuts and the use of inferior, synthetic materials to maintain margins. When sales continued to sink, General Mills sold the crocodile to a sportswear marketer for $50 million in 1985—about one-eighth of gross revenues of the brand just five years earlier.

The brand continued to flounder because the new owner followed a similar strategy: discounts, inferior materials, and market-share madness. *Forbes* magazine later dubbed it the "anemic alligator."

As the brand became synonymous with low prices and low quality, a buyer at Barneys, the trendy upscale New York department store, had a now famous conversation with Ralph Lauren. Mr. Lauren's business was then mostly focused on up-market men's ties, but he was willing to listen. The Barneys representative wanted a high-quality, all-cotton replacement for the ailing alligator. Forget about volume, the buyer said, just give a shirt that can justify a high price. Soon Lauren's polo pony was trampling the alligator. The U.S. owners of the Lacoste brand had essentially ceded a highly profitable market to an upstart tie-maker—a disastrous decision that is proving very hard to undo.

Meanwhile, Lacoste, with its partner firm, Devanlay S.A., bought back the U.S. license for $30 million in 1992 and, after a cooling-off period of several years, reintroduced the classic polo shirt with a "made in France" label. Its strategy is to charge more than the prices of its competitors, precisely to restore the brand's prestige. Today the crocodile's sales are on the rise—and Lacoste is off the market-share treadmill. The French company earns solid profits on its shirt sales. Saks Fifth Avenue is once again selling the shirts. But it can never undo all of the harm of past market-share mistakes. As late as 2002, Polo continues to earn the lion's share of profits in the high end of the $2.8 billion market.

THE INTERNET VERSUS MARKET SHARE

Now, more than ever, market-share strategies make little sense. The benefits of size, such as they are, are slipping away. Technological change is sweeping away many of the supposed advantages of market share. Even the economies of scale that often come with a large market share may not confer much benefit in the near future—the Internet allows smaller rivals to band together, win volume discounts, and achieve "virtual scale." Consider a joint venture between Honeywell and General Electric Co. known as MyAircraft.

MyAircraft.com is a website that allows buyers to pool their orders. On MyAircraft, several buyers can set common technical specifications and bundle their orders together.

MyAircraft's potential power could make real trouble for companies focusing on market share alone. When a large number of orders are pooled, both the buyer and seller should benefit from economies of scale. Each can amortize their costs over a larger number of units; factories can run at full capacity with fewer changeovers; and so on. Prices can be lower while margins could stay roughly even. In theory and practice, everyone wins.

MyAircraft helps GE keep its aircraft engine factories busy, while its customers receive lower prices. Who loses? The aircraft part makers who counted on market share and a multitude of small orders to keep prices high.

But pooling orders also creates a kind of market power. Once the number of industrial buyers working together is large enough, the balance of negotiating power shifts to them. On Volumebuy.com and other sites, ordinary consumers can do the same thing. Want a discount on a cruise or a Palm Pilot? This website bundles together thousands of buyers and wins volume discounts from manufacturers.

For managers, this situation—what economists call "monopsony," meaning one buyer, the flip side of monopoly—poses two sets of questions. Executives ought to ask: What would happen if our customers banded together? In industries—everything from coal to bananas—where sales are driven primarily by price, collective purchasing could increase the pressure to slash prices and, eventually, costs.

But Web-based buyer's unions can demand more than just lower prices, especially in the business-to-business arena. Imagine a number of regional auto-parts retailers getting together to face down a large parts maker. After winning some price cuts, they might demand speedier deliveries, more integration between the store's inventory and the supplier's, a better return policy, and so on. Suddenly, selling to a heap of small fry can be like selling to General Motors. Now imagine this trend rippling across every business sector in the world.

Actual size is about to meet what I call "virtual size." Suddenly all of that hard-won market share can be had, by your rivals, with a few clicks of the mouse. Whatever the outcome, the assumed *automatic* benefits of size are going, going, gone.

Virtual size will upset the settled ways of the market-place and rob "dominant" firms of their "rightful" place. Large corporations usually have three suppliers, at least in strategically important areas. There's the primary supplier—picture an industry giant with a well-known brand; a secondary supplier, an established player who is there in case the leader can't deliver in terms of quantity or quality; and a third supplier, perhaps an upstart, whose role is to put pricing pressure on the other two.

Now along comes a Web-based buyer's union to threaten the supplier hierarchy. Ordinarily, edging aside the established supplier wouldn't be worth the trouble for a big business. Why disturb a long-standing relationship for some temporary price savings? But when the cost savings produced by a buyer's union become big enough, corporate inertia dissolves.

Virtual size can steal away the power of market-share giants—without taking on the corresponding costs of bulking up. Indeed the smaller members of the buyer's union may benefit disproportionately. And the market-share giants will suffer disproportionately. Suddenly, actual market share does not look so attractive.

THE BIGGER IS BETTER MENTALITY

The appeal of market share is partly explained by corporate psychology. "They feel embarrassed pounding their chest and saying that their company is the most profitable. It's nicer to say that they have the most market share," says George Mason University economics professor Tom

Rustici, "especially if they aren't that profitable." He should know the mind-set; he once ran a supermarket chain in Kansas City.

In fact, Mr. Rustici knows something about turning the bigger is better mentality against itself. As the head of a family-run supermarket chain in Missouri, he got a call one day from a competitor. Would Mr. Rustici meet him at a nearby diner? Sure, he said. He was surprised: The city's supermarket owners almost never talked to one another.

When he got there, the room was filled with local supermarket operators gathered around a table. They were scared. Wal-Mart was opening a giant supermarket nearby and could seize almost half the market. Mr. Rustici was determined to keep his stores, but some talked about selling their family-owned stores. Others wondered aloud how long they could stay in business. "They are gonna cut prices to the bone," one said.

As he drove back to his main supermarket, Rustici began to develop a plan for beating the new giant. He called his staff together. He told them about the Wal-Mart and then said: "If I hear about any of you going to the new Wal-Mart—even on the weekend—you'll be fired immediately." Some employees tittered. They thought that Mr. Rustici was trying to stop them from shopping at the competition. But he had a larger goal: He didn't want them to go to the megastore and be afraid of its size; he wanted them to think about how to beat it.

For the next month, Mr. Rustici and his employees examined every price on every product in the store. They negotiated discounts with their suppliers, where they could. They cleared the shelves of products that didn't sell well or didn't earn good margins. "We needed to make every inch of shelf space as profitable as possible," he said. He conducted a top-to-bottom review of every aspect of the business. He pared costs and eliminated waste. He even changed the way his butcher cut the meat. He vowed to make his stores as efficient and competitive as possible.

Then, about a month later, in February 1990, the Wal-Mart supermarket opened. The megastore soon developed a commanding market share, as other stores lost sales. But Mr. Rustici's tiny, two-store chain held steady.

Then, after another month, Mr. Rustici walked up to a stock boy and said: "Let's go for a ride." When they pulled into the Wal-Mart parking lot, the boy looked scared. "Don't worry. You're not getting fired," Rustici told him. "We're here to do a little market research."

Together, they wandered the aisles of the massive store. The Wal-Mart store could fit two of Rustici's super-markets onto its gigantic floor and still have room to spare. They looked at prices for leading items. Then Mr. Rustici noticed that baby formula was on sale—for a price lower than he could buy it from his supplier. This is where the power of large volumes and market share hit home. But he refused to give up. He picked up a case and asked the stock boy to grab another.

"Are you sure?"

"Yeah, come on."

After they paid for the formula, they drove back to Mr. Rustici's store and put it on the shelf—at the regular price. Next, he phoned his distributor. It turned out that the distributor was also selling to Wal-Mart—at the same price that it was selling to him. "We can't even buy it from the factory that cheap," the distributor insisted. So Wal-Mart's supermarket had a classic loss leader, Mr. Rustici realized. He organized groups of employees to surreptitiously buy as many cases as they could. All were resold at Mr. Rustici's store at the usual price. His margins had never been so good.

Soon he began targeting other loss leaders. Although these bouts of guerrilla capitalism helped, paying attention to customers, improving efficiency, and keeping prices competitive (without sacrificing margins) are what allowed Mr. Rustici to sustain his business in the face of a much-larger, better-financed competitor.

Within a few months, Wal-Mart's Kansas City hypermarket was in trouble. The Wal-Mart Hypermarket closed and was converted into a Wal-Mart Supercenter in 2000. The most likely problem was that the supermarket's low prices were attracting customers but the loss leaders did not generate enough sales of other profitably priced products. "All you have to do is think about your customers and your profit margins," Mr. Rustici said, "and you can run circles around any large market-share business."

His training as an economist and his entrepreneurial determination helped him outwit one of the largest, most profitable companies on the planet.

MARKET LEADER VERSUS PROFIT LEADER

What Mr. Rustici knew was that market-share enthusiasts overlook the difference between being market leader and being profit leader.

Market leaders focus on market share. They reward their divisional managers and sales forces on winning or keeping market share.

Profit leaders focus on profits. Their goal is to earn a

higher rate of return than an investor can earn in an index fund or a certificate of deposit. They reward their managers on the basis of net profits, not sales volume. We'll take an in-depth look at market leaders and profit leaders in Chapter Five.

Any discussion about market share naturally leads to this question: What about General Electric? GE is consistently one of the most profitable companies. Check out GE's profit performance since 1980—the chart looks like a profile shot of the Himalayas. Yet its announced goal is either to be number one or two in a particular line of business or to get out.

GE is one of the most misunderstood business models in the world today. GE has only one goal, one true north: sustainable, above-average return on capital invested. Its market-share analysis is really a metric for deciding to invest in a sector, not an organizing principle of corporate strategy.

Indeed, Jack Welch's real contribution was transforming GE from a market leader to a profit leader. A close study of the Welch way reveals how your company can travel the same path.

Finally, some contend that high-tech or information age businesses need to focus on market share. They usually cite something economists call "network externalities." The classic example is the telephone: The more people who have telephones compatible with yours, the more valuable your phone becomes to you. The same is true of e-mail, instant messaging, cell phones, fax machines, word-processing software, even credit cards. Therefore, Microsoft and Visa have to achieve dominant market share just to remain viable businesses.

This is a profound and complicated argument—and a

sign of the changes sweeping the global marketplace. Coming technologies will create ever more network externalities—when your new, Web-linked refrigerator wants to talk to the supermarket's mainframe, it had better use one of the more popular software languages. But, as Microsoft and Visa learned, they are in a new competitive environment. We'll learn the new rules in Chapter Six.

This book is a road map away from the ruinous focus on market share to the twenty-first-century corporation: networked, focused, and intensely profitable. It is packed with cautionary tales of companies seduced by market share and with case studies of phenomenally successful firms that focus on profit.

CHAPTER TWO

Hard Lessons: Why Gillette Is Smarter Than AT&T

We've just run the largest controlled experiment in the history of the world—involving more money and more people than the Manhattan Project and the moon shot *combined*.

The world invested hundreds of billions of dollars in high technology—everything from wireless outfits and telecom-equipment makers to software writers and dot-com purveyors. The hypothesis that we were testing in this global laboratory: Does market share matter?

Most of these new enterprises shared at least two characteristics: a belief that market share was the best path to success and that profits, if they mattered at all, could wait. With the crash of the dot-coms—"the tech wreck" as the British press aptly called it—it's hard to believe now just how confident so many entrepreneurs, venture capitalists, and new-economy gurus were about market share and how dismissive they were about the more pedestrian emphasis on profits. To get a full appreciation for their ebullience, their absolute certainty that market share was all that mattered, let's dial back into market-share madness.com—the biggest case of share mania in modern memory. Consider just two examples, torn from the pages of the then-hot dot-com magazine *Business 2.0.*

"WHAT'S MY ROI ON ECOMMERCE? ARE YOU CRAZY? THIS IS COLUMBUS IN THE NEW WORLD. WHAT WAS HIS ROI?"

—ANDY GROVE, CEO INTEL

"NO, NEAR-TERM PROFITS AND A BLACK BOTTOM LINE DO NOT MATTER. IN FACT, STIFLING GROWTH IN ORDER TO PRODUCE SHORT-TERM PROFITS WILL ALMOST CERTAINLY LEAD TO A LESS VALUABLE BUSINESS."

—RICH SHAPERO, MANAGING PARTNER, CROSSPOINT VENTURE PARTNERS

"Do profits matter? No. The ability to lose a lot of money before making even more used to be the provinces of very big companies," says Nicholas Negroponte, a leading high-tech business guru affiliated with MIT's Media Laboratory. "Note that at the product level, strategies for market domination have been around for ages."[1]

Well, Mr. Negroponte is right about one thing: All those dot-commers with dollar signs in their eyes were just doing what big businesses have done for decades. And that's the problem.

The new-economy mavens followed an old corporate strategy—they were hooked on the same old ideas revered by the old-economy giants that they hoped to displace. And what have we learned from the abysmal failure of that strategy? After all, all that money should buy us at least a little wisdom. Let's take a hard look at the case *for* market share.

THE CASE *FOR* MARKET SHARE

All of the arguments for market share are as old as the dot-commers were young.

One of the earliest studies of the connection between profitability and market share was conducted by University of California–Berkeley professor Joe S. Bain in 1952.[2] Mr. Bain was testing this hypothesis: "the size of profits or profit rates [varies] to the degree of seller concentration within industries"—in other words, whether a few high-market-share firms together earn more money than a collection of low-share firms. Surveying forty-two industries, he found that profit rates were higher in sectors in which the biggest eight firms accounted for 70 percent of the market. This view quickly became part of the conventional wisdom, which proved very hard to dislodge.

(At the time, few noticed a line Bain had inserted near the end of his famous article: "Absolute size of firm did not appear to be significantly related to profit rates in any simple fashion.") In other words, while Bain thought a small collection of high-share firms could earn big profits, he wasn't certain that one big firm could do so. But strategists, executives, and consultants ignored this small but vital distinction.

The definitive study in favor of a market-share-centered strategy was published in 1975. That may sound like a long time ago, but "Market Share—A Key to Profitability" is still assigned reading in many business schools and was recently collected in a book called *Marketing Classics: A Selection of Influential Articles.*

Many Web entrepreneurs studied the theory in business school—the 1990s entrepreneurs were among the best-educated start-up artists in American history—and those who didn't study it no doubt absorbed it from those who did. Market-share mania seemed to pop up in every cubicle from Silicon Valley in California to Silicon Alley in New York.

The primary author of that classic study was a Harvard Business School professor named Robert D. Buzzell, and for the famous article he was joined by two coauthors. Professor Buzzell went on to publish several other studies on market share, and his thinking has largely shaped what amounts to the debate over market share as a component of business strategy. (One can still download Professor Buzzell's seminal work from the Harvard Business School's website for $5.95 a pop. Harvard isn't giving the article away to build market share; in fact, it is almost certainly priced way above marginal cost.)

Reading Professor Buzzell's work, one is immediately struck by two things: He seems to have gradually eased off his landmark claims about market share, without admitting as much, and he considers the benefits of a commanding market share to be largely automatic for big companies. (The dot-commers believed these things, too.)

These two key assumptions undergird virtually every argument for pursuing a market-share strategy.

SECOND THOUGHTS?

At first, Professor Buzzell seemed boundlessly confident. His 1975 work was expansive and powerful. He began his famous article thus: "It is now widely recognized that one of the main determinants of business profitability is market share. Under most circumstances, enterprises that have achieved a high share of the markets they serve are considerably more profitable than their smaller-share rivals. This connection between market share and profitability has been recognized by corporate executives and consultants, and it is clearly demonstrated" by Professor Buzzell's research.[3] He continued: "There is no doubt that market share and return on investment are strongly related."[4] No doubt, he wrote. Yes, he wrote: "no doubt."

In a moment, we will examine the substance of his claims, but for now let's pay attention to his confident style. By 1981, as the amount of contrary evidence was building, Professor Buzzell had trimmed his sails a bit. "Market share *helps determine* [emphasis mine] business performance." That is a long way from "no doubt."

Interestingly, Professor Buzzell's more careful phrasing, which appeared in a 1981 research paper called "Successful Share-Building Strategies," was in the lead paragraph of a much larger study. In that paper, he examined 2,000 companies—nearly four times the number surveyed in his earlier work. A larger sample size should have made him more confident, not less. Unless, of course, the larger sample produced a more heterogeneous result than expected.

Admittedly his later work still strongly ties market share to profitability. Yet scholars rarely like to admit that they might have overstated the case, especially when their work is widely recognized and praised, as Professor Buzzell's work was, and deservedly so. But this stylistic retreat should be kept in mind when we turn to the evidence about market share and profits.

There is another interesting undercurrent in Professor Buzzell's work and those of many others; it is the idea that the benefits of market share are largely automatic. Since firms with large market share can have a larger number of customers or larger production runs, they can lower per-unit costs. They can more broadly spread their advertising, accounting, and other overhead costs and use their bulk to demand volume discounts. These benefits, while quite real, are *assumed* to be realized. These benefits simply come with size, an automatic little gift.

Little thought is given to the idea that potential benefits are not always turned into actual benefits, in the real world. One is reminded of the joke about an economist and a mechanical engineer trapped on a desert isle. Their only bit of food is a can of tunafish and they have no can opener. The mechanical engineer gets to work, trying to devise a wave-driven can opener. "Let me try first," says the economist.

"Yes?" says the engineer expectantly.

"First," says the economist, "assume a can opener . . ."

This gap between theory and practice also needs to be kept in mind.

BUZZELL'S THEORIES

Now let's turn to the five major arguments that Professor Buzzell and others make for market share—all of which are far from proved. They are either assumed into existence or are of trivial importance in the teeth of real-world competition between aggressive firms.

Myth Number One: Leadership and Market Power. In theory, the dominant firm—the one with the most share—can set the prices. The Big Kahuna gets to call the tune. Or to cite a favorite aphorism of market-share mavens: "The guy with the biggest slice [of the market] never goes hungry." The rest have to carve up his scraps.

Of course, large-share firms with the bulk of an industry's production capacity certainly can lower prices. They can flood the market with excess supply and hammer down prices. But can they use the same power to *raise* prices—which is supposedly the benefit of market leadership?

Although market leaders might be able to boost prices by reducing marginal profits, it is hard to see why they should try to trim margins to increase sales. If the percentage reduction in price per unit is larger than the percentage increase in market share, the firm loses money. This is usually what happens.

Precious little evidence exists to show that large-share firms can raise prices and make them stick. By raising prices, a large-share firm gives its competitors what consultants call a "price umbrella"—smaller rivals can either maintain prices and capture some of the business that the so-called dominant firm has chased away, or they can raise prices by a smaller fraction than the "price leader" and earn fatter profits. Sure, this benefits competitors, but what does the big dog get out of it? Not much. In fact, he often loses precious market share in the bargain.

The dirty little secret is that there is no such thing as market leadership based on share alone. Yet we see large-share companies try to use their "market power" all the time—with little to show for it. This is the game that AT&T plays with MCIWorldCom—in fixed lines—that British Telecom plays with Vodaphone in wireless, and that nearly every phone giant plays with independent service providers in North America and Western Europe.

Surely some dominant firms have raised prices and had them stick. But take a closer look and market share has little to do with it. Usually big-share firms that are able to raise prices for their products—and keep them up—offer something else, such as a unique benefit or feature that the competition cannot easily imitate or counter through clever marketing. Gillette—a market leader—was able to win higher prices for its Mach III razors because the product is vastly better than anything the competition offers. The market research showed and experience proved that customers would pay as much as three times for the Mach III than for the competitors' disposable razors. But, again, this was a function of the product's unique value proposition—not Gillette's market share.

Perhaps the current, hypercompetitive market doesn't allow "market leadership" based on market share; you might say, but if conditions changed, then perhaps the behemoths could command prices. Let's think about this a moment. Imagine if antitrust laws didn't exist, and there were no barriers to growth in market share. Welcome to the world of the so-called robber barons, who should be the most powerful case for market share translating into "market leadership" and pricing power.

American Sugar Refining owned 98 percent of all sugar refining capacity east of the Rocky Mountains in the 1890s. Even Bill Gates never wielded such market power. And the sugar company was selling a staple. Consumers couldn't make do with last year's model. They needed to keep buying sugar. So American Sugar should have had unbeatable market power—it should have been able to set prices.

American Sugar tried to use its size to reduce sugar production, thereby hiking prices. Result? Lower-priced sugar poured in from California, Canada, and even the Caribbean. Despite decreased production in American Sugar's home market, prices fell. Within two years, prices were lower than before American Sugar's birth. It kept buying up competitors—hoping to make their market-share, pricing-power strategy work. It never did.

American Sugar, thinking it could dictate terms because of its size, gave the competition an opening, allowed them to establish a beachhead, and ended up weaker. So much for large-share firms' alleged pricing power.

But some lessons have to be continuously relearned. Consider the merger of Usinor SA of France, Arbed SA of Luxembourg, and Aceralia Corporacion Siderurgica SA of Spain, now known as New Co.: The steel giant hopes to be big enough to set prices. After all, it is the world's biggest producer of steel.

New Co. will control almost half of the production in Europe. A cinch to boost prices, right? Not a chance. Competitive steel plants crowd the horizon of central and eastern Europe, Belarus, Russia, and the Ukraine.

They're ready to take New Co.'s customers away. "They are living in cloud cuckooland if they think they can have any pricing power in Europe," Commerzbank analyst Peter Dupont told me. "If they raise prices, imports will be sucked in."

The world market sets prices, not regional Goliaths. No firm can ever become mighty enough to beat back a world of competitors, who usually pay lower wages, enjoy a better relationship with key customers, or boast a friendly government willing to underwrite their losses in the name of "national pride." Self-declared market leaders are only fooling themselves.

Myth Number Two: Size Naturally Creates Higher Returns. The second case for market share is simple, widely believed, and wrong: As market share increases, so do profits. "Except perhaps in embryonic or rapidly expanding market environments, competitors ranking lower than fourth or fifth must increase market share," Professor Buzzell writes.[5]

In the 1970s, Professor Buzzell developed a formula to support this idea: "On average, a difference of 10 percentage points in market share is accompanied by a difference of about 5 points in pretax ROI."[6]

Whatever the merits of Professor Buzzell's formula, it certainly doesn't apply in today's hypercompetitive, globalized economy.

Some large-share firms do earn more than their nearest rivals, but most do not. Increased profitability is not the automatic prerogative of size, and share is not even a good rule of thumb for finding the most profitable firm in a particular line of business. Remember, seven times out of ten, the most profitable firm was not the one with the most share, as Windermere's research shows.

Myth Number Three: Economies of Scale Kick In. The third argument for market share is based on "economies of scale"; or, the more widgets you make, the cheaper they are per unit. "A business with a 40% share of a given market is simply twice as big as one with 20% of the same market, and it will attain, to a much greater degree, more efficient methods of operation within a particular type of technology," write Professor Buzzell and his coauthors.[7]

Again, consider the good professor's assumptions. An enterprise with 40 percent of the market *might* be able to wring more concessions from its suppliers, workers, and bankers. But it might not be as energized to do so as its smaller rivals. And its suppliers, workers, and bankers might prevail in resisting its cost-cutting entreaties—after all, the megafirm is "big enough to afford it." It would be fairer to say that higher market share gives firms the *opportunity* to win such efficiencies.

Economies of scale don't come automatically from bigger market share or greater volume. Most firms squander executive energy on market-share growth, instead of exploiting the economies of scale that are supposed to come with it. "They think of market share as an end in itself," Jack High, a former Harvard Business School professor, told me. "It is not."

And economies of scale have a seldom talked about flip side, what economists call "diseconomies of scale." As firms become larger, they put on layers of management and take on other costs—more plants, higher training costs, larger debt service. Eventually they have too much overhead to compete in certain market segments. Higher market share yields higher returns only if margins are maintained—something that becomes progressively harder as the firm stretches to reach more and more of the market.

And, too often, managers forget about the law of comparative advantage and price. There are always markets that are cheaper for a niche player to serve than a mass producer. Why go after the next 10 percent of market share when the necessary price reductions will bring demands for discounts from the 30 percent you already serve? And, among that 30 percent, there are almost always customers who cost more than they are worth. In both cases, attempts to maximize market share mean lower profits.

Myth Number Four: The Experience Curve Improves Efficiency. Then there is the so-called experience curve, pioneered by the Boston Consulting Group in the late 1960s. The theory is quite sound. Total unit costs should decline as a company's output grows because it is learning more about making its product or delivering its service. This experience allows them to become more efficient. Doughnuts are cheaper by the dozen only when bakers use the knowledge gained from increased production to shrink costs. More market share means more production, which in turn means that larger companies are learning faster than their smaller rivals. Thus they should be able to cut costs more steeply than their smaller competitors. At least in theory.

The reality is quite different. Again, these efficiency gains are far from automatic. Suppliers don't see the market-share gains in the newspaper and phone your purchasing department with offers of larger discounts. These cost cuts must be won through negotiation—and suppliers want to maintain their margins, too. In manufacturing operations, increased output usually means reconfiguring and enlarging the production process—which takes time, energy, and money. Meanwhile senior management is demanding that the plant move more product out the door. As a result, wringing cost savings out of the production process is often an afterthought. In a distribution enterprise, the logistical problems of increased business can overwhelm managers; who has time to try to trim costs? And, in a service business, the experience curve tends to flatten out fairly early. How many law firms are more efficient with 750 lawyers than they were with 600?

The experience curve sets cost-savings targets that are, more often than not, not reached because no single manager or group has responsibility for meeting them. Instead, managers do what they can where they can and hope the big picture takes care of itself. Firms that treat the benefits of the experience curve as targets and reward managers for reaching those targets, rather than as automatic prizes for enlarging themselves, tend to do better in realizing the benefits of size. But, in practice, few firms bother.

The experience curve is a valid insight, but it needs to be viewed as a target for increased efficiency—not an automatic prize for getting bigger. Indeed, even the Boston Consulting Group seems to be rethinking the importance of market share in relation to the experience curve.

Carl Stern, the president of the Boston Consulting Group, visited Hong Kong in February 2000. During his visit, he talked to a reporter for the *South China Morning Post,* one of Hong Kong's largest newspapers. The reporter asked if he'd change anything about the understanding of the experience curve.

"I would change the share thing," Stern said. "Not in all industries is market share the right thing to have on the horizontal axis [of the Growth-Share Index]. You want something around competitive advantage or a particular driver around competitive advantage for your portfolio, and that might or might not be market share."

The translation from consultantese: A diversified company, trying to choose between investing in two different divisions, shouldn't necessarily rely on market share as a guide. You want to look at the fundamentals (cost advantage, market growth, and so on).

The bottom line? Even the company that invented the experience curve, it seems, no longer considers it a major reason for chasing market share.

Myth Number Five: Quality Management Leads to Growth. In this argument, higher market share attracts exceptional managers. How do we know that the managers are exceptional? Why, their market share is growing! But aside from the obvious circularity of the argument, there is an unstated assumption: Companies with growing market share are believed to have and to attract better managers than firms with static or shrinking market share. Indeed, this notion is sometimes cited as one of the key reasons managers need to focus on market share.

Some companies with growing market share *do* have exceptional managers. Many large-share firms are also the most profitable in their chosen line of business, as the Windermere study cited in Chapter One shows. But, chances are, what draws prime managerial talent is not a firm's market share but managers' own opportunities at the firm for advancement and enrichment, as well as a certain freedom to reach corporate goals as they see fit.

This was amply demonstrated by the droves of experienced managers who left the old-economy companies to work for Internet start-ups. Of course they left for the possibility of instant riches, but more control, increased responsibility, and the entrepreneurial spirit also played a part. Many large-share firms simply don't offer such opportunities and freedom. As for those that do, corporate culture is more likely the cause than simply a large market share.

Besides, market-share growth is a poor proxy for quality management. After all, 70 percent of the firms with the largest market share in their line of business do not earn the highest return on assets, according to the Windermere study. If market share were an essential ingredient for attracting the best managers, then these firms would presumably be doing better—not worse—than their competitors.

And there are good reasons to believe that large companies see their size as a deterrent to wooing the best managers—something that must be compensated for with a dynamic, open corporate culture. Excellent managers are often repelled by a large company's bureaucracy and its resistance to change. That is one reason that General Electric Co. devotes a lot of executive energy to retaining and rewarding its best leaders and clearing away bureaucracy.

What does Welch have to say about bureaucracy?

"We cultivate the hatred of bureaucracy in our Company and never for a moment hesitate to use that awful word 'hate.' Bureaucrats must be ridiculed and removed. They multiply in organizational layers and behind functional walls—which means that every day must be a battle to demolish this structure and keep the organization open, ventilated and free. Even if bureaucracy is largely exterminated, as it has been at GE, people need to be vigilant—even paranoid—because the allure of bureaucracy is part of human nature and hard to resist, and it can return in the blink of an eye. Bureaucracy frustrates people, distorts their priorities, limits their dreams and turns the face of the entire enterprise inward."[8]

And Welch understands the importance of retaining top talent:

"The top 20% [in terms of ability, not position] must be loved, nurtured and rewarded in the soul and wallet because they are the ones that make magic happen. Losing one of these people must be held up as a leadership sin—a real failing."[9]

But part of retaining top talent is creating a positive corporate culture at every level. As Welch notes, a manager who makes the numbers but doesn't share GE's values, someone who achieves but does it "on the backs of people, often 'kissing up and kicking down,'" must be found and removed "because they have the power, by themselves, to destroy the open, informal, trust-based culture we need to win today and tomorrow."[10]

It is a healthy corporate culture, not market share, that attracts talented managers, argues Jack Welch—who ran a company with both a strong culture and a large market share.

Case Study: DaimlerChrysler

DaimlerChrysler's obsession with market share, among other factors, has helped drive away many quality managers. Chrysler's star managers, the ones who made the number three automaker number one in profits—before the sale to the German automaker—have fled. Even the legendary "car guy," Bob Lutz, left his beloved Chrysler shortly after the merger. Virtually none of the original management team remains three years after the megamerger. The sheer scale of the merged automaker meant that many decisions were transferred to senior executives in Stuttgart, Germany. Like American officers in Vietnam, they had to wait weeks for a decision from a faraway bureaucracy and found themselves bedeviled by growing mounds of paperwork. Frustrated, they began looking for a way out.

Through it all, Daimler executives talked confidently about market share and economies of scale. Daimler itself was once quite profitable, before it bought Chrysler and a large stake in Mitsubishi. By 2001, only vehicles with the Mercedes-Benz nameplate made money.

In fact, some of Daimler's problems—the ones that scare away top talent—come from its massive size and a focus on market-share growth. The Chrysler division has been too slow to trim costs and couldn't kick the old Detroit habit of rebates and other sales incentives. This trains customers to wait for bargains, creates volatile shifts in consumer demand, and shrinks profit margins by bribing customers in order "to move the metal," as they say at Chrysler's headquarters in Auburn Hills, Michigan.

Then the remaining Chrysler executives decided to

set a "stretch" target for market share. The automaker, which usually has about a 14 percent share of the target, hopes to reach 20 percent by 2005.

Plans to buy market share get expensive—fast. In some cases, Chrysler was spending $3,000 in sales incentives per vehicle sold. Chrysler's marketing costs (including all of those rebates, cash giveaways, and low-interest loans), as a share of revenue, expanded to more than 21 percent in the first quarter of 2001, up from 13.3 percent in the first quarter of 2000. Losses grew. By contrast, Ford spent only 12 percent of its revenues on marketing—while earning strong profits. By 2001, Chrysler reduced its rebates and began paring costs—but the damage was done.

Other costs also exploded. Chrysler's break-even point reached 113 percent of its plant capacity in the dark days of 2001. Chrysler simply could not make enough cars to break even. Chrysler's cost structure had been rising before the merger, but costs worsened considerably afterward. Chrysler moved to having the most workers per percentage point of market share in 1999, up from having the fewest per point of market share in 1996. But after the automaker's historic tie-up with Daimler, costs kept climbing.

DaimlerChrysler CEO Jurgen Shrempp has vowed to defend Chrysler's 14 percent market share in the United States at all costs. Meanwhile, Chrysler's red ink is drowning the global automaker—which had to post huge losses. Chrysler, once very profitable on its own, announced plans to eliminate 26,000 jobs by 2003. Some 20 percent of Chrysler's workforce were encouraged to take early retirement or laid off. Six assembly plants will be shuttered over the same period. The most optimistic projections anticipate at least two years of losses at the automaker; total losses could reach $10 billion by the end of 2002. Meanwhile, the best managers keep walking out the door. If you were a top-flight manager, would you stick around?

All of this money and time sacrificed on the altar of size. Still, Mr. Shrempp defiantly tells the press: "We are not changing our strategy." Maybe not, but Daimler-Chrysler's experience should put to rest the idea that maintaining market share is the best way to attract or keep the best managers—sometimes it is the most effective way to drive them away.

LEARNING FROM EXPERIENCE

As we have seen, all the supposed benefits of market share are hollow. Leadership and market power; size inevitably yielding higher returns; the vaunted power of economies of scale; the experience curve; and size attracting the best managers—all of these benefits of size are either highly questionable, very hard to achieve, or simply assumed. This leads us to a crucial question: Can a company reverse course on its market-share strategy and earn above-average profits?

The dot-commers ran out of time, money, and investors' patience. But one classic old-economy company points out the folly of market share and the path to recovery.

Case Study: Boeing Co.

Boeing is easily the biggest maker of planes in the world. On any given day, more Boeing aircraft—everything from the venerable 727, the workhorse 747, and the large

777—are in the sky around the world than all other makes combined. But the giant plane maker almost crashed in the mid-1990s—and its brush with death taught it some painful lessons about market share.

The downward spiral began in early 1995, when Boeing executives were stunned to learn that its rival, Airbus Industries, had booked more orders than Boeing the year before. The then-Seattle-based plane maker usually took 70 percent of the world's orders for new planes; it took less than 50 percent in 1994.

Many insiders described what followed as "panic." Some feared that Airbus had dethroned the plane maker and the 1994 orders would soon give their European rival a dominant position in the aircraft business. Some Boeing executives had come over from the McDonnell Douglas merger: They didn't want to go back to working for a number two plane maker. Others feared that Boeing— with some 70 percent of the industry's production capacity—would be left with idle plants, a large redundant workforce, and a sagging stock price. Nightmare scenarios whirled around Seattle like a freak wind shear that could suddenly smash an aircraft into a mountainside.

In this superheated atmosphere, Ron Woodward, Boeing's head of the commercial aircraft unit, decided to reengineer Boeing's production process. He wasn't going to lose another year—or another sale—to Airbus.

Little thought was given to the possibility that Airbus's success was a fluke—a combination of a plane-order boom, subsidized loans from European governments, and a runway full of below-cost or thinly profitable sales.

Boeing was so determined to keep its leading market-share position that it decided to take on its subsidized European competitor. Almost overnight, the company's mind-set shifted. Boeing became obsessed with market share. "A company that was once nervy enough to assume it could sell all of the planes it chose to make switched to thinking it needed to make all the planes it could sell," wrote the *Wall Street Journal*'s Holman W. Jenkins Jr. Maintaining market share became its highest priority.

But to accept every possible order, Boeing would have to fundamentally change the way its 200,000 workers built planes—in one year.

Incredibly, Mr. Woodward largely pulled off his ambitious goal. Gone were laboriously hand-drawn blueprints and paperwork that accompanied every part and every design alteration. Boeing also shrank the number of customizable features—which were costly to stock and track. The aircraft company no longer offered 109 shades of white paint; now it allowed only 20. While many of these changes were long overdue, the suddenness and the vastness of the change in strategy and the change in the production process shocked Boeing lifers.

Then came an even bigger, market-share-driven change. Mr. Woodward also wanted to triple production to 550 planes per year. Union officials say that internal plans were even more ambitious—some 660 planes per year. Either way, Boeing's desire to regain market share made it act like a passenger trying to stuff a steamer trunk into an overhead bin.

The new airplane production process wasn't even ready for a test flight before its pilots expected it to do three times as much as they were accustomed to doing. Bottlenecks formed and delays grew. Customers fumed as costs climbed.

Still Boeing refused to throttle back sales. It might lose market share.

Many of those sales weren't worth much. Prices had to be slashed for some buyers, who then demanded costly customizations. Others required expensive financing packages. Boeing ended up with orders for almost 1,000 planes while facing record losses.

The smiling, bespectacled Mr. Woodward was fired. Boeing announced layoffs, trimmed other costs, and began taking only truly profitable orders. But it had a hangar full of bad orders to clear out. Boeing posted a loss in 1997, its first in 50 years.[11]

Boeing's next chief executive, Phil Condit, so far seems to have resisted the siren call of market-share mania. When Airbus announced a new superjumbo jet in 2000, Boeing refused to match them in an expensive race. When he visited the offices of the *Wall Street Journal Europe,* I mentioned that Airbus might be taking orders for the new jet at a loss. Mr. Condit only smiled.

Meanwhile Airbus continues its government-subsidized approach of selling new planes at or below cost. The headline-making Singapore Airlines order for the new Airbus Superjumbo—the largest commercial passenger aircraft ever designed—is probably not profitable. Airbus said that it needs a minimum of $225 million per plane to break even on the A3XX. Consultants and industry experts estimate that the planes were sold for less than $160 million—a loss of more than $65 million per plane. Airbus refuses to describe the sales as either "profitable" or "unprofitable." But it is almost certainly losing money to build market share.

Now, Boeing is too smart to play that game. Mr. Condit repeatedly told me that Boeing "aims to be profitable on every single product line." Left unsaid: Market share will take care of itself. Whatever the benefits of having the most market share are, they pale in comparison to earning sustainable profits on everything sold. Boeing snapped out of its market-share tailspin before crashing into the tarmac.

But it's not easy to change old dogmas. Boeing arrived at the 2001 Paris Air Show determined to put the air show order theatrics to an end. The company is determined to stop saving airplane orders just so they can be lumped together and announced as part of the air show extravaganza. "We are not going to ask airlines to wait [to reveal orders] so that we could make a big deal about it. We just decided that this is silly," said Randy Bessler, vice president of marketing for Boeing Commercial Airplanes.[12] At the show, Airbus announced 175 orders for jets. Boeing announced 3. The press snickered.

So is Boeing worried that it announced only three "orders" at the Paris Air Show? Hardly. Boeing's second quarter net income was up 35 percent in 2001. Boeing's aircraft sales dropped almost 6 percent in the second quarter of 2001, but its earnings rose 8.3 percent. Its profit margin increased to 10.2 percent from 7.6 percent a year-over-year.

Many aviation industry analysts aren't worried about Boeing's commitment to making a profit at the expense of market share. "Over time Airbus might even pull ahead, but is that such a terrible thing? As long as Boeing is making enough money from every airplane they sell, that's the most important thing," says William Loh, an aviation industry consultant.[13]

Yet how many new- and old-economy outfits will follow Boeing's lead?

CHAPTER THREE

Fatal Seduction: Why the Myth of Market Share Has Seduced Everyone from the Robber Barons to Your Boss

How did we get here? How did "market-share madness," as more than one analyst has called it, reach such a crescendo that executives, entrepreneurs, and investors were willing to spend perfectly good money to get it and to accept staggering losses or drastically reduced margins just to keep it? In short, who created the myth of market share and why does it exert such a powerful hold over so many business leaders?

The answer, like Caesar's Gaul, is in three parts: It is a matter of business history, constituencies (both inside and outside your company), and financial incentives.

THE HISTORY OF MARKET SHARE

Let's begin at the beginning, with history. The great economist John Maynard Keynes once observed that today's leaders are often unknowingly in the grip of "some long defunct economist."

That is certainly the case with market share and today's decision makers. The myth of market share was forged in the fires of the industrial age and put on a pedestal by a group of intellectuals and regulators who were hostile to big business.

In the late nineteenth century, the market-share strategy was so simple that it sounded like common sense. The more you sell, the more you earn. By the 1870s, the race was on to grow bigger and sell more. And it seemed to work. Companies that poured steel, purified aluminum, built railroads, drilled oil, dug coal, and pounded out metal cans made mounds of money.

Soon they discovered that size had other advantages. Large scale gave manufacturers the ability to be the sole supplier, at least the primary supplier, to other enterprises, who were themselves bulking up. That meant that large suppliers could expect to grow in step with their large customers.

The so-called robber barons were not the relatively disinterested professional managers of today; they owned large and often controlling blocks of their companies. They constantly demanded that every conceivable cost be wrung out of the production process. One morning, Standard Oil executive owner John D. Rockefeller famously walked on to the factory floor and began testing the machinery for soldering oil cans. By trial and error that morning, he learned that the cans didn't need the forty welds they were receiving, but only thirty-eight. Over a large run, that small savings would add up. That became the new standard for Standard Oil.

Few advantages of size were left unrealized. Standard Oil built its refineries and self-insured against loss. It was cheaper than paying premiums to insurers. When Rockefeller was told that coopers charged $2.50 to make each barrel, he decided to make his own. He bought white-oak-tree plantations, built kilns to dry the wood, and used the company's wagons to haul the timber to Cleveland. "There, with machines, he made the barrels, hooped them, glued them and painted them blue," write Donald Boudreaux and Burton Folson.[1] Barrel costs fell to 96 cents each.

Large orders from suppliers meant volume discounts; large shipping volume translated into lower transportation costs and so on. Things became cheaper by the dozen, and cheaper still by the hundreds and thousands. Larger revenues meant more money for research, which meant more improvements in products and more refinements in the production process. As volume grew, costs per unit fell. Size seemed to "lock in" customers because greater scale gave an illusion of permanence and the strength of a trusted brand name. Plus, there was the phenomenon of "customer inertia"; businesses and consumers rarely shifted suppliers in those days. So bigger companies were also better able to attract the best managers. Bigger *was* better—more cost-efficient, more profitable, more innovative—and produced higher-quality products. But why don't these benefits accrue to large enterprises today, provided that they have energetic managers?

Times change. These massive steel age enterprises—picture tens of thousands of employees toiling under factory roofs that could be measured in acres—were different from contemporary business in a number of important ways: They had few competitors and many customers. Demand was greater than supply; therefore their primary problem was building capacity to serve voracious demand. It was the economy of need, not an economy of desire.

On the other hand, customers, both businesses and consumers, had relatively little power. There was little foreign competition. Access to capital was difficult for new entrants, but became easier with greater scale. Competition was based mostly on price, and innovation spread slowly, due to relatively poor communication and transportation infrastructure. There was a mass market—customers of all types, in all regions of the country, wanted identical or substantially similar products. Finally, product-oriented services—such as warranties, repairs, and upgrades—were rare. In short, the robber barons faced a completely different competitive environment than today's titans.

In that unique moment—at the birth of the modern corporation—chasing market share might have made sense. Making steel, mixing chemicals, laying rail lines, refining oil—these were large, capital-intensive enterprises that offered nearly identical goods. In that world, at that time, the winner was the company that sold the most stuff. Thus the mantra was born: "Sell the most and the profit will follow."

These giants seemed to be textbook examples of the power of a market-share strategy to generate large returns and provide a sustained competitive advantage. But it was short-lived. Even during their era, the myth of market share was already becoming a myth.

Let's look at some of the companies that exemplified the market-share strategy in the early days:

- Union-Pacific Railroad. Though Union-Pacific and other railroad Leviathans had enormous market shares—including monopolies on key routes—they were eventually unable to control prices. Average railroad freight rates fell to 20 cents per ton per mile in 1900, from $1.75 per ton per mile in 1865. Many railroads were sold or broken up or bankrupted. The survivors found themselves in a low-margin commodity business.

- American Can dominated the metal-container business by 1901, owning 90 percent of capacity in the can business. It hoped to finally take advantage of its massive pricing power. It raised prices by 25 percent and quickly lost 30 percent of its market share. It kept buying up its rivals, but prices quickly returned to premerger levels each time. The giant can maker was left with a mountain of debt and no pricing power. Then the U.S. Justice Department sent it a subpoena. Soon the trustbusters stopped it from buying its rivals.

- Standard Oil. Standard Oil once seemed so big that it threatened not just other competitors but even the prospect of competition itself. When John D. Rockefeller's Standard Oil had won 90 percent of the oil market in 1897, it had, through scale efficiencies, pushed down the price to 5.9 cents per barrel of kerosene from 58 cents in 1873. Internally, its refining cost of kerosene fell to 0.45 cents per barrel from 3 cents per barrel in 1870. This wasn't altruism. The oil giant would have charged higher prices if it could have, but, even with its large market share, it was threatened by competition.

Then it was broken up in a landmark 1911 case. But the courts merely added insult to injury; the market share of the once-mighty Standard Oil had already fallen to 64 percent in 1911, before the breakup.[2]

- U.S. Steel. Andrew Carnegie, who dominated the steel industry, was unable to stop the plummet in the price of steel rails to $17 per ton in 1898 from $160 per ton in 1875—a decline of 89 percent. In 1901, the market share of U.S. Steel was 61 percent; by 1920 it was 39 percent.[3]

What went wrong?

Problem Number One. The competitive environment changed, shifting the balance of power. By 1900, all of the defining factors of the marketplace had been altered—but the market-share strategy had not. By then, there were many competitors, and customers were more demanding. Supply was now equal to demand; therefore, serving the customer was at least as important as building capacity. And the power of customers, both businesses and consumers, was greater than that of producers. Foreign competitors crept into the market. Access to capital was still difficult but becoming easier for small and midsize companies. Competition had shifted from price to benefits and features; innovation was spreading more quickly, due to improved communication and infrastructure—much of it built by the companies that once thrived on market share alone. The market was becoming more differentiated—customers of all types, in all regions of the country, wanted goods designed for them, not some anonymous "mass market." Finally, services—such as warranties, repairs, and upgrades—were becoming a key competitive advantage. The robber barons soon realized that they either had to change their strategy or get overrun by rivals who were not beholden to outmoded theories. And, of course, the regulators were after them.

Problem Number Two. Managers did not distinguish between correlation and causation. In other words, they believed that just because one event (growth of large companies) was followed by another event (rising profits), then therefore size made profits. It didn't, as they learned by the end of the so-called Gilded Age. But that is a painful lesson that managers seemed doomed to relearn.

Problem Number Three. With the advantages of size come the disadvantages (as discussed at the end of Chapter Two). Beyond a certain point, the disadvantages are greater than the advantages. Even in those days, technology had a way of transferring the benefits of scale to much smaller competitors.

Cost control is vital. But it becomes much harder with size. Why? A company with ten employees may need only one manager, while a company with one hundred employees can make do with only ten managers. But one thousand employees need more than a hundred managers, managers for those managers, regional vice presidents, as well as an extensive accounting department, a legal team, a purchasing operation, a shipping and receiving unit, and so on.

Problem Number Four. Innovation wasn't enough. Standard Oil transformed the oil business by discovering some 300 petroleum by-products and pioneering uses for them, including lubricating oils for machinery, petroleum jelly for worn hands, and paraffin for candles.[4] But Standard Oil's legions of chemists were no match for the global marketplace, which was crowded with firms that specialized in packaging, distributing, and customizing these discoveries, as well as discovering innovations of their own.

Problem Number Five. The robber barons didn't realize that the birth of the industrial age was a unique period in economic history. It can't happen again; things only begin once. The strategies of those early days simply will not work in our time or in any conceivable point in the future.

The robber barons didn't even know that the strategy they were following was based on something called "market share"—the term probably didn't exist yet. These captains of industry were just blindly trying to make money. When something worked, they kept doing it until it didn't. Then, they tried something else. There were no consultants or business school professors or self-styled business gurus to give them theories. That came later.

In the beginning what we call market share seemed to work. That was the beginning of the seduction. But market share became more alluring when it became a myth, a founding story that explained the growth of giants and the secrets of commercial success.

Who created this myth? Interestingly, it wasn't the early capitalists, but their critics. Just like the term *capitalism* itself, which was coined by Karl Marx and Friedrich Engels, the phrase *market share* was created by those opposed to big business. They created the theory to explain the behavior they abhorred, not to teach managers to maximize shareholder value. But this inconvenient fact has faded into the mists of history.

Seduction requires mystery, and the origins of both

the phrase and concept of market share are shrouded in mystery. So if we are to understand market share's spell over so many business leaders around the world, we need to do a little detective work.

A LITTLE WORD HISTORY

The phrase *market share* entered the English language sometime in the 1940s. The scholars at the *Oxford English Dictionary* track when words and phrases enter the English language. The first known citation of the term, in print, appears in 1954, in an American academic journal, the *Journal of Industrial Economics*. This is startling and strange.

After all, the component words *market* and *share* have been English for more than 700 years. The first recorded use of the word *market* appears in a copy of a charter written in 1053 and variations of the word can be found in postclassical Latin in the early Middle Ages, as well as in most European languages, including German, Dutch, Flemish, French, and Swedish in the twelfth century. It became a common English word—with current spelling and meaning—in the thirteenth century.

The word *market* was popular enough to appear in bits of business advice and in the plays of William Shakespeare. Medieval business leaders were often counseled: "You may know how the market goes by the market folks." In other words, the best market intelligence is gleaned by watching the behavior of buyers and sellers, not by the elaborate theorizing of observers. Not exactly the kind of advice proffered by consultants, who love their theories and surveys, but solid advice nonetheless.

In Shakespeare's play *As You Like It,* Act III, Scene 5, Rosalind counsels Phebe, who is considering a proposal from a man whom she does not love: "Sell when you can: you are not for all markets." Product managers, who need to time the market, say the same thing today.

The word *share,* with its current meaning, is almost as old. It appears in documents stretching back to the thirteenth century. Earlier uses of the word refer to the part of a plow (then known as the shear) that cuts through and divides the soil into furrows. That sense survives as the word *plowshare.* Later, of course, *share* came to stand for a part of a thing.

But until the twentieth century no one ever thought to put the two words together. Again, there appears to be no reference in print to "market share" until 1954. Businessmen have been calculating their total sales for eons and estimating the number of potential customers in a given market for centuries, but they apparently never talked about their market share. Why?

That question leads into another direction, also veiled in secrecy. The *concept* of market share appears to date from the late nineteenth century.

The men of the industrial age did not think about market share, exactly. They thought about the number of miles of rail that they laid or the tons of steel poured. They thought about return on capital invested. They even thought about how big the market might be for, say, a cleaner-burning illuminating oil, such as kerosene. (Kerosene was much cleaner burning than whale oil.) In short, they thought about inputs and outputs, dollars and cents.

Even when they compared themselves with their competitors, they did so in terms of industrial capacity—the amount of product that their busy plants could churn out—or in terms of gross revenues. They certainly thought about profits. But not how big their slice of the market was compared with those of competitors.

Indeed, there was no way for those titans of industry to know what their market share was. There were few publicly available, audited financial statements and even fewer market-research outfits. (All of those estimates of nineteenth-century market share were devised by academic economists, decades later.) No one really knew what the size of a particular market was—some even said it was infinite or unknowable, because consumer preferences could not be accurately predicted then. (Some would say the same today, but that is another subject.)

Yet the concept of market share began to creep into public discussions as the critics of the robber barons multiplied. We'll meet some of those critics, the mothers and fathers of market share, in a moment. The point here is that market share did not begin as a business concept, but as a means of criticizing businesses. And the idea of market share certainly wasn't developed to teach businesses how to become more profitable.

Perhaps the greatest critic of the robber barons was the famous muckraking journalist Ida Tarbell, a hawk-faced woman with a burning hatred of a man she never met—John D. Rockefeller. A relative of hers ran a tiny oil refining business in western Pennsylvania in the 1890s. He was run out of business by the vastly larger, much more efficient Standard Oil. Mr. Rockefeller's company bought up the competition and consolidated the staff. Anyone who wasn't needed was fired and inefficient plants were ruthlessly closed. He used his large production capacity to win volume discounts from railroads and shipping outfits—transportation costs were a large component of the final price of oil in those days. He also used his immense production capacity and giant cash flow to borrow rivers of capital from Ohio banks at fairly low interest rates. No competitor could match Standard Oil, which by the turn of the century was the nation's largest oil company.

Ms. Tarbell wasn't amused. She and other critics worried about how much of the market Mr. Rockefeller controlled. Implicitly, she worried about market share. She saw it solely as a measure of the hated Standard Oil's dominance. Her fiery criticisms, published in New York newspapers, eventually attracted the attention of senators and presidents.

Meanwhile, U.S. Senator William Sherman, the younger brother of General William Tecumseh Sherman, the legendary Indian fighter, was thinking about the same issues. The younger Sherman didn't want to fight business like his brother fought Indians; the senior senator from Virginia thought of himself as a friend of enterprise. But he too was mesmerized by the size of the new industrial enterprises. These giants had too much of the market, he said, and would crush the little guy. He wrote the nation's first antitrust law, the Sherman Act. Thanks to its brevity and its vague language, this elastic law is still one of the most widely cited in federal antitrust lawsuits.

Then, in 1901, a gunshot vaulted a little-liked vice president into the Oval Office. His name was Teddy Roosevelt and he quickly made it clear that he thought that market share mattered. He launched forty-four federal efforts to break up businesses with large market shares—an average of seven per year. This came as a shock to the robber barons. Until then, the antitrust laws were applied mostly to labor unions, which also had a large share of the labor market. (Today unions are generally considered to be exempt from antitrust laws.)

Over time, the theory of the regulators and critics prevailed over the experience of managers who had seen it tried and failed. Later, the market-share proponents had an easy way of dismissing executive experience: You're just not doing it right. Others believed the critics of Standard Oil's dominance and tried to follow their "strategy," without, of course, drawing the fire of regulators.

What explains the staying power of this theory? Why has this strategy outlived every one of the conditions that made it plausible? Why do so many businesses continue to cling to it, using it and refining it, when it has failed for the very companies who first developed it? In short, why is the market-share strategy so seductive?

Myths spread and develop staying power when they are written down, written about, and debated. Businessmen, who saw the market-share theory tested in the crucible of experience, wrote internal memos and didn't debate their corporate strategies in public. So much of the early, hard-won experience of the market-share strategy was lost to history. On the other hand, the critics who concocted market share were gifted writers, like Ms. Tarbell, who published in leading magazines, gave speeches, and wrote books. Thus they were able to influence the next generation of managers. And ultimately their thinking became an important way in which business looked at itself.

Myths flourish when they are embraced by interest groups. The myth of market share flourished as it won over new constituencies, people whose livelihood depended on it, at least in part. These constituencies are still found in nearly every major company today. There are two kinds of constituencies: internal and external.

INTERNAL CONSTITUENCIES

The first is what I call "internal constituencies." These are groups within the corporation that favor market-share growth over maximizing profits. These constituencies are not bad; they just have their individual incentives misaligned with the companies' long-term profitability. Let's look at who they are:

- *Division managers* with a large number of old plants or legacy systems under their control. The last thing they want to hear is that market share doesn't matter. It is their best justification for maintaining the status quo.

- *Union leaders.* Their members judge them based on how many jobs they can deliver, not how high the company's stock price climbs. While much of the workforce might be producing thinly profitable products, that's not the union's problem. And if the company does produce a large profit, that could put a labor leader in a real tough spot, too. If the company is so profitable, can't they pay workers more or hire more people? Better to keep the factories humming and not worry too much about the bottom line. Again, market share is the best reason for maintaining the status quo.

- *The sales force.* First, high market share seems like a good selling point to potential customers—could so many purchasing agents be wrong? Second, market share is really about sales volume. More sales equal more commissions and more bragging rights. And if most of those sales aren't profitable, so what? Their job is to sell.

If you weigh the institutional barriers to improving a product against the weak resistance to trimming margins, you can see why market-share theory is so attractive to executives. Given internal resistance to change, it is easier to buy market share than to earn profits.

EXTERNAL CONSTITUENCIES

• *Consultants.* Outsiders also play a role in the myth of market share. They studied market-share theory while earning their high-priced degrees and now they have a high-priced strategy for growing it. Market-share's analysis and growth is a great product for consultants to sell—it is difficult to increase (think of the billable hours), time-consuming (ditto), and has few internal foes. Besides, executives are often mesmerized by it— why not sell them the services they want? If profits sink, they'll have another plan to offer. To cite again Professor Buzzell's influential *Harvard Business Review* article: "This connection between market share and profitability has been recognized by corporate executives and consultants . . ."

• *Analysts.* A large or a growing market share is a good reason to recommend a "buy" for a company's stock. Remember, "buy" recommendations tend to outnumber "sell" recommendations by a factor of eight to one. And

market share is a good-sounding reason for recom-
mending a stock. Analysts usually report to fund managers, who need to diversify their portfolios across a
range of sectors. What if no company in the sector
looks promising? Recommend the biggest—you can always sell later. So analysts help keep share at the top of
executives' minds, by asking about it.

- *Media.* Journalists have editors. Pitching a story about
  a large company is always an easier sell, as are stories
  about growing or shrinking market share. But that
  doesn't mean the coverage will be positive.

- *Customers.* Few purchasing agents want to take risks.
  Why not order the products and services that already
  command a large market share? At worst, they will buy
  exactly what their competitors are buying—and be no
  better and no worse off. And, for consumers, buying a
  product that has a large amount of public acceptance
  seems comforting. Of course, if the product or service
  doesn't deliver, customers will flee just as quickly.

All of these constituencies keep the myth of market
share going. But, as we shall see in the next chapter, there
is a cost to bowing to their demands: the long-term health
of the firm.

YESTERDAY'S STRATEGY, TODAY'S COMPETITION

Today, market-share strategy has many refinements, but
in essence it is the same. And yet the global marketplace
today has changed even more than at the turn of the twen-

tieth century. Technology and the historic rise of investment capital—think of the nation's more than 1,500 venture-capital funds, with tens of billions of dollars at their disposal—have further reduced barriers to entry. Free trade and globalization have brought in new competitors. And, in most industries, the capacity to produce is greater than current demand. All of the relevant characteristics of the market have changed—but again the market-share strategy has not.

As a result, in such a competitive environment, great companies can die—if they try to hold on to market share. These companies have clung to their faith in the old religion of market share—and it is bringing them closer to death.

Consider AT&T, which was founded in the days of the robber barons; it was one of the nation's first incorporated businesses. And, for years, it has tried to defend an outdated market-share strategy. The world's largest telephone company has shed divisions and slashed payrolls. But new entrants like MCIWorldCom and Sprint have kept AT&T's margins low. AT&T and its former research arm, Lucent Technologies, have together lost more than $350 billion in market capitalization in 2000 alone. Now, AT&T is breaking itself up into separate companies—for the second time in five years—in hopes of restoring profitability. Best of luck to them.

So businesses are competing in the twenty-first century using a strategy forged in the nineteenth century and refined in the twentieth century. It's not a recipe for success. The goal of increasing market share makes companies do strange and reckless things. It is a beautiful siren calling the ships to the rocks. What happens to the companies that heed its call?

CHAPTER FOUR

Makin' the Numbers: Why Market Share Leads to Dangerous Discounts, Wounded Brands, and Foolish Mergers

In the mid-1950s, Sony was trying to make its mark with one of the world's first transistor radios, the TR-55. The company knew its chances of becoming a big business hung on the fortunes of its tiny radio.

Sony had overcome a lot of hurdles to get to this point. Ministers at the all-powerful Japanese government agency, known as MITI, laughed when they heard of Sony's plans to make radios—and initially refused to allow the company to transfer the Japanese yen necessary to license the transistor technology from RCA. The technology itself was difficult and, at the time, no one in the world had ever manufactured enough quality transistors to support industrial radio production. And small radios were unheard of—except in Dick Tracy comic strips.

Then there were the business challenges. Sony had no U.S. distributor and its original name—Tokyo Tsushin Kogyo—was hard for Westerners to pronounce. The

Sony name was created by merging the Latin word *sonus* (meaning sound) with the then-hip American term *sonny boy.*[1]

So Akio Morita, one of its founders and later its chief executive, was dispatched to New York in 1955. He brought along a stack of radios and a keen sense of urgency.

Soon he had a dilemma. A Bulova watch company purchasing agent, who had seen the new radios, made Mr. Morita an offer. He would take 100,000 units—a huge order worth more than the entire market capitalization of Sony in 1955—but only if the radios were sold under the Bulova name. "I'm sure you understand," he said, "nobody has ever heard of Sony."[2]

If Mr. Morita took the deal, no one *would* ever hear of Sony. All of its work would strengthen the Bulova brand.

There was another problem: Sony was struggling to produce 10,000 radios per month. Its costs would grow sharply if it took the order—and its margins would fall, perhaps to zero. It meant hiring more people, a larger investment in capital equipment, higher supply costs, costly alterations to the production line, and larger shipping and inventory costs. So Sony would enjoy market share, but perhaps no profits.

So Mr. Morita couldn't afford to take it and couldn't afford not to.

He cabled the board of directors for guidance. They strongly and repeatedly told him to take it. What happened next is in dispute, but it appears that Mr. Morita turned down the offer on his own. It was "by no means the last time that Morita would defy his own board of directors," writes John Nathan, who produced a video documentary history of Sony and wrote the definitive book-length account of the company's rise.[3] Mr. Morita wanted profitable growth and to build a world-class brand—not to produce commodity electronics for others.

Mr. Morita's gamble paid off. Sony quickly became a leader in radios and, later, in television sets and other consumer electronics. Today Sony sells some $65 billion worth of consumer electronics around the world, second only to Hitachi's $67 billion. As for the Sony name, analysts put its value alone at $16 billion. Mr. Morita's bold move to turn down the Bulova offer looks better all the time.

And who has ever heard of a Bulova radio?

But let's pay attention to what makes this story surprising and important. Most companies are so busy chasing large orders, catching the big fish, that they're willing to hook the big guy with low margin, low return "promotional," or "introductory," prices. What about raising prices later? Fugetaboutit. Higher prices might lose the big account. Few managers would have the courage of Mr. Morita to patiently explain the rationale for a higher price or turn down a big offer—wouldn't it be easier to get the sale and try to raise prices later? And managers might talk about maintaining their margins, especially on the conference call with analysts and institutional investors, but in the hurly-burly of deal making, defending the margin is often sacrificed to getting the sale. And why do they want the sale so badly? Market share.

In this chapter, we will look at all of the strange dances and odd contortions companies put themselves through just to woo market share.

KILLING BRANDS TO GAIN SHARE

General Motors recently offered a new indirect discount: a free safety and security system worth $1,500. This comes on top of other rebates that total $2,000 on some models. The catch for the company? The OnStar System was once supposed to be a strong reason for consumers to pay more for GM luxury cars. Now it's just another freebie. "People used to be proud to own a Corvette or Cadillac; now they just wait for the price wars," sighed one Virginia car salesman. Once again, market-share mania—GM was afraid of losing its 28 percent share of the American car market— had led to discounts and wounded brands. Never mind that GM has been shedding market share for decades, while following the same strategy.

These stories aren't unusual. Nearly every major company is killing its brands with discounts. Foolhardy executives are undoing one of the great marketing achievements of the twentieth century: the creation of brands, products, and services that sell based on symbolic value, not price alone.

Rampant price cutting is sapping the strength of brands that companies have spent many decades and billions of dollars building; they're turning product and service brands back into commodity businesses. Commodities, like steel and coal, are virtually identical goods that compete mostly on price. That means razor-thin profit margins and vicious price competition. Look at the coal or steel industry lately? Lots of bankruptcies and teary trips to Washington and Brussels asking for protection. Why would anyone want to join that parade?

Discount-crazy managers should think about the message that "bargain prices" communicates about brands. Customers wonder: If all of the products are the same, why not buy the cheapest? Industries that rely on discounts train consumers to expect price concessions. The airlines have coached consumers to wait for price wars and super-savers while the World Wide Web has made price-based shopping easy.

With discounts and promotions, all that companies have accomplished is to turn smooth sales charts into violent waves: The peaks are during the fire-sale prices and the troughs during periods of "normal" prices.

The retailing sector has gradually worked itself out of this ulcer-inducing cycle of sales volatility with "Everyday low prices" and other techniques. But some manufacturers never seem to learn.

Why do businesses resort to reckless discounts? They offer a variety of rationales: We're just trying to meet our quarterly numbers, we're trying to build brand loyalty, we're just chopping prices to match our competitors'. It all boils down to efforts to defend or enlarge market share.

None of these excuses hold up. Discounting shrinks profit margins, which squeezes quarterly returns. And if you get a sales bump (unlikely when everyone else is doing it), all you've done is move future sales into the present. After the low-return, high-volume mountain comes the valley of low volume and low return.

Brand loyalty is based on the idea that a product or service is uniquely better and different, not cheaper. Discounting thus erases a key difference with the competitors' products. This is supposed to be high strategy?

Then there's the persistent idea that you must lower prices when your competitors do. Most marketers act as if consumers decide to buy their brand based solely on price. They're wrong. Few people have the time and energy to comparison shop. Who drives to four stores to get the best deal on a bar of soap? Only 15 percent to 35 percent of consumers (depending on what they're buying) consider price to be the chief criterion for selecting a product, according to a recent study by Copernicus, a marketing investment strategy group based in Auburndale, Massachusetts. More than 60 percent of consumers don't consider price at all. Nearly 80 percent cannot correctly recall (within 10 percent) the price they paid for a particular product in the last seven days. They do remember the brand, though. Hmm . . .

When customers do think about prices, two factors drive their thinking: the amount of disposable income they have and how much they care about the product category, according to the Copernicus study. Some people are emotionally involved with great brands like BMW, Sony, and American Express. Some small part of their identity depends on buying the brand that they consider the best. Some people order top-shelf scotch, while others save a few cents and order a no-name "rail" drink.

Buyers have different sets of categories that matter to them. Some think a toilet paper brand is very important but a credit card brand isn't. To some, a BMW is the "ultimate driving machine"; to others, a car is just a means to get "from point A to point B." In short, each type of product has its share of "high-involvement" buyers, who care about quality and brand, and "low-involvement" buyers, who care mostly about price. In every product category, high-involvement buyers outnumber price-fixated shoppers by more than two to one, according to studies.

Businesses that focus on the needs of high-involvement buyers can consistently charge higher prices while their rivals offer similar products at discounted prices and earn lower margins.

But attempts to build market share run counter to efforts to build a brand relationship with high-involvement buyers. Why? Because reaching high-involvement buyers takes a lot of time and money, it is a real effort to get them to switch brands. (But when they switch, they tend to stay loyal.) So wooing the price shoppers seems like the quick and easy way to grow market share. But the instant that prices move, so do these buyers. This traps market-share companies in a low-price spiral—while driving away high-involvement buyers, who find that their needs are no longer being met.

LOWERING PRICES

Cutting margins to boost volume invites competitors to match the new low price. If the competition's cost structure is the same or lower, then a pointless price war follows. This periodically grips the airline industry and the beverage (both beer and soft drinks) industry, and it is what automakers do repeatedly. "It is easy to sell minivans," one analyst told me grimly, "when you put $2,000 in the backseat of each one."

But there is a better way. Consider the retail gasoline industry. The conventional wisdom is simple and simply wrong: Since all fuel is the same, the only way to compete is on price. This should be an area that vindicates the market-share maniacs, but it isn't. After months of research, Mobil identified the needs of high-involvement buyers: fast, friendly service, brightly lit stations, and clean toilets. Mobil decided to put the service back in service stations—and charge a bit more for its fuel.

The result? While 1997 sales fell 2 percent for the industry as a whole, Mobil enjoyed a 3 percent increase in sales. That is a big boost in a highly competitive business. Mobil's retail gasoline sales revenue remained steady in 1998, as total industry sales revenue—hammered by discounting—declined another 3 percent. (After the Exxon-Mobil merger, this successful strategy was put on hold. As a result, the merged company ceased to be a profit leader in its industry.)

While there are some good reasons to lower prices (such as sweeping technological change that lowers production costs across the industry), marketers need to learn from Mobil. Firms should give customers a definite reason to buy a product, beyond price. Once they have identified what sets their product or service apart, they must clearly communicate this benefit to customers through an integrated marketing, advertising, and sales plan. Here is a hint: Target the high-involvement buyers.

When you discount, you're telling high-involvement buyers that they're wrong to care so much about your brand. You should hope that your competitors keep discounting their products. Let them sell commodities—while you build a brand. "Now is the time to remind your customers why your brand is worth more. Make communicating the importance of your brand a key part of your marketing strategy," says Robert Shulman, co-founder of Copernicus. (He is now chairman of Markitecture, a Norwalk, Connecticut–based marketing consulting outfit.) "Let your competitors cut their prices to build share. They know what their products are really worth."

BAD MERGERS

Another quick way to build market share is to buy your competitor's customers—by buying your competitor. This is the story behind many of the mergers of the last few years.

Sometimes this works brilliantly. In overlapping markets, consolidation of the back office functions—accounting, legal, purchasing, and so on—can often create significant efficiencies. Product offerings and service agreements can also be rationalized. Mergers can also boost global market share by helping companies enter new markets while building on a solid foundation of established brands, loyal customers, and savvy local managers. Too often it does not work out that way.

Eighty-three percent of cross-mergers "were unsuccessful in producing any business benefit as regards shareholder value," according to a recent study by KPMG, which canvassed 107 board members who participated in the top 700 cross-border deals (by market value) between 1996 and 1998. KPMG then measured the value of the merged firm one year after the tie-up.

Why didn't these mergers produce value? Because dealmakers focused too much on financial or legal issues, instead of operations and people. Acquirers who postponed resolving the differences in corporate culture to the postdeal period were much more likely to fail, according to KPMG. The few who, at the beginning, addressed different corporate values—those messy cultural traits that define large businesses in the minds of their employees—were 26 percent more likely than average to succeed. More often, the guys in the executive suite are arguing over which one is going to be chief executive of the merged business. When they decide to become "co-CEOs" you might as well short the stock.

Mergers may produce larger market shares but, all too often, don't produce significantly higher returns. There usually isn't much value beyond the mild economies of combining the "back office" functions. The hoped-for "synergies"—often invoked to sell the deal to investors—never seem to arrive.

Why do mergers fail? Economies of scale are not an automatic result of combining two titans but must be realized through painstaking paring of redundant personnel, functions, and processes. When Ford bought Jaguar in 1989, Ford planned to share platforms—the car's underlying skeleton—between Jaguar and Lincoln, its upmarket U.S. brand. This prompted years of retooling and harmonization, which cost Ford hundreds of millions. The Jaguar unit didn't start to show profits until 1996. After a false dawn of profitability, Jaguar was losing money again in 2000.

Half-realized economies of scale can create opportunities for competitors. When BMW bought Rover, executives predicted that economies of scale would help turn around the ailing British automaker. Right. Modernizing the venerable Rover's plants and sharing parts with BMW proved to be costly and unwieldy. Despite economies, Rover continued to drain BMW, while smaller Japanese companies like Mitsubishi and Nissan entered the sport utility market and seized the lower end. Meanwhile Ford and Lexus lured away upscale Rover buyers.

As losses mounted, BMW sold its Rover division. Today it is one of the world's most profitable automakers—despite its relatively small size. Its corporate strategy has changed. Growth through acquisition has been replaced by maintaining margins, controlling costs, and leveraging its powerful brand through careful line extensions. Thus, in 2001 BMW unveiled a new station wagon and a brand new sport-utility vehicle. But others have yet to learn from BMW's experience.

Or consider Volvo. The conventional wisdom is that companies that make fewer than two million cars per year are too small to be competitive. But this is nonsense. Volvo produces only 400,000 cars a year and is one of the world's most profitable automakers. It sold its car division to Ford Motor Co. not out of desperation but to concentrate on its even more profitable truck business. "It is very possible to remain a profitable and specialized car producer," says Volvo Cars then president Tuve Johansson. "Size does not correlate to profitability."

Even when mergers result in genuine cost advantages and other synergies, these tie-ups often spur competitive responses. Consider GM's 1990 purchase of a 50 percent stake in Saab AB. Despite some early economies of scale, Saab failed to become the low-cost leader in its category because rivals cut costs even more ruthlessly. Volvo aggressively trimmed payrolls, reengineered processes, outsourced, and improved their products—just to beat Saab. As a result, profits for Saab failed to materialize for seven years. Meanwhile, Volvo's car division became immensely profitable—and was eventually snapped up by Ford for more than $6 billion in cash.

Dennis Kozlowski, former chief executive of Tyco International, is a master at creating shareholder value through mergers and de-mergers. "The key thing I've learned is that acquisitions work best when the main rationale is cost reduction. You can nearly always achieve them because you can see up front what they are. You can define, measure and capture them. But there's more risk with revenue enhancement [buying market share]; they're much too difficult to implement."[4]

To succeed, mergers must be quick and spur internal changes. Mr. Kozlowski argues: "A very interesting statistic I once read says that people are normally productive for about 5.7 hours in an eight-hour business day. But anytime a change of control takes place, their productivity falls to less than an hour. That holds true in merger situations. Inevitably, people immediately start thinking about themselves. So moving fast and getting the right people in place are extremely important. At Tyco, we look to the companies we acquire to provide those people. We present our objectives and our philosophy, and we look for the people who respond. Often, it's not the top executives but rather the people under them who are the quickest to understand and embrace the new philosophy."[5]

ENTERING TOO MANY MARKETS

To grow share, companies often try to compete in every niche in the market and at every price point.

Companies can't resist filling in the gaps of product offerings—even if there isn't a hole in the market. Managers at those would-be dominant firms seem to succeed at first, but soon learn the hazards of trying to be all things to all buyers.

DaimlerBenz was a world leader in creating large luxury cars with fat profit margins. So why did Daimler decide to enter the market for small, spartan economy cars with negative profit margins? In a word, market share.

The company is publicly committed to having a product in every possible automotive product line in the world.

Daimler introduced the flat-nosed two-seater, called Smart. Sales barely topped 120,000 Smart cars in 2000—much less than the projected 200,000. Sales have been disappointing, even in Europe, where gas prices are in excess of $4 per gallon and annual car registration taxes are often based on engine size (thus making small cars much cheaper and therefore very attractive). Also, nearly all Europeans adore small cars because they are easier to park in Europe's meandering, narrow cobblestone streets. (The Smart has failed U.S. collision tests and is not available in America.)

The entire Smart car is roughly the size of a car door on an American luxury automobile, and barely fits two people. It has no backseat and a trunk the size of a doormat. "Smart is no good for young families or, indeed, for anyone with more than one friend," noted the *Economist* dryly.

The small-car market has never been a high-margin product segment in Western Europe and North America. Meanwhile, Japanese, Italian, and French automakers have cornered the small-car market in the developing world. As a result, the tiny Smart car is a big money loser. Daimler has lost more than $1 billion and counting on Smart—while most of its target market turns up its nose.

BONEHEADED BRAND EXTENSIONS

Another favorite way to chase market share is with "brand extensions."

This probably seems like a smart idea in the conference room. You have a great brand and want to launch it into a new customer segment. With luck, you'll get some sales, some top-line growth to brag about, and some market-share gains.

Sometimes this works really well. Take Procter & Gamble's launch of laundry detergent with bleach added. It had clear benefits for consumers: no more lugging bleach bottles to the cash register, and no more measuring cups full of bleach. The result was cleaner clothes and fewer bleach spots. What's more, it was a *believable* brand extension—the detergent that cleans your clothes now does it better.

Some brand extensions are laughably bad. A.1. is America's number one steak sauce. Then someone noticed that people are eating less beef and more chicken. Meanwhile, the baby boomers are aging and becoming more health conscious. Add to that the number of beef-related health scares in the United States and Europe. A.1.'s market was slowly shrinking. Something had to be done to reduce these ominous long-term trends.

So A.1. cooked up A.1. poultry sauce: a chicken sauce with the brand name of a steak sauce. Customers were confused, and sales were disappointing. It was pulled off the market.

Most brand extensions are not so sensible (like putting bleach in detergent) or so risible (like trying to sell a new chicken sauce under a name that symbolizes beef, salt, and fat). Most brand extensions are merely bone-headed attempts to boost market share. These moves can do companies a lot of harm.

Consider the rise and fall of the Miller Brewing

Company. In the late 1960s, Miller was America's number three beer maker and its sales were going flat. It was a small division in a sprawling global conglomerate known as W. R. Grace.

Top management had little time to think about its brewing operations and had little experience in consumer products. Then in 1969, Philip Morris bought the beer business. After all, they knew a lot about marketing a mildly addictive product and building a brand.

They quickly repositioned Miller High Life as "the champagne of beers." Instead of addressing women and high-income men, who are generally not big buyers of beer, the new Miller team targeted working-class men, who buy most of the beer in the United States. They unleashed a new line of television commercials featuring men in hard hats and oil workers battling a blowout. "Now it's Miller time" was the slogan.

It worked beautifully. Miller rose to be a close second in nationwide beer sales in 1980, from being a distant third in 1970. Sales were growing and the future looked bright. Maybe they were about to knock the number one brewer, Anheuser-Busch, off its perch.

But it was not to be. Miller's mistake? They did a smart thing in a dumb way. They got into the brand-extension game.

In the beginning, it looked like genius. They launched Miller Lite—the first successful national low-calorie beer. Timing was perfect: Jogging was becoming a national obsession and Jane Fonda's workout tapes were a hit. Miller got all the fundamentals right, too. Its distributional strength carried the new brew to new drinkers (especially women), the advertising was funny and on target ("Everything you always wanted in a beer—and less" and "Tastes great—less filling"), margins were good, and the price was right.

Miller Lite sales took off like a rocket and left Miller High Life in the dust. By 1985, Lite was outselling its parent brand, High Life. Miller Lite had pushed High Life aside as the second most popular beer in America. The legendary marketing expert Jack Trout chronicled what happened. Sales of Miller Lite surged to 19 percent of the U.S. beer market in 1986, from 9.5 percent in 1978. By contrast, Miller High Life sank to 12 percent from 21 percent over the same period. "When you chart the rise of Miller Life it's almost a perfect 'X,'" notes Mr. Trout, in his book *Big Brands, Big Trouble.*[6]

Still Miller refused to learn that brand extensions can sap the strength of existing brands and stall a fast-growing business. The 1990s brought waves of new brand extensions—everything from Miller Reserve Light to Miller Clear. Most belly flopped and those that survived went on to further wound the Miller brand. Miller had, in the end, become a portfolio of hard-to-distinguish brands that together fail to deliver growth.

Bottom line: If you want to roll out a completely new product, give it a new brand name.

There are smart ways to extend a brand—by keeping it within a very narrow band. Consider Procter & Gamble's Tide division. Tide, America's most popular laundry detergent with 40 percent of the market, has created sixty variations of its core product. All have a consistent theme. There is Tide Free (no fragrance), Tide Kick (which includes a nozzle to apply soap directly onto clothes), and so on.

FORGETTING CUSTOMER SERVICE

Increasing market share means wooing more customers or enticing existing customers to buy even more. So why do so many firms ditch customer service to boost market share?

Consider the cable modem business. Cable modems were sold to the public as superfast Internet connections. No more waiting a seeming eternity for Web pages to load. The cable modem demonstrations showed Web pages zipping across computer screens at the click of a mouse—clicking on to new websites was like changing channels on a television set.

But there was a catch—the more users the cable companies signed up for the cable modem, the slower the service would become. Why? Because cable operators were too busy signing up customers to add new nodes to meet demand. The more users per node, the slower the service. Add enough users and the cable modem was slower than the old telephone dial-up modem that crawled along at 56K. The value proposition vanished, but cable companies were too busy signing up customers to notice.

Many customers had an experience similar to that of David Kong in Alexandria, Virginia. He subscribed to a cable modem service offered by Jones Intercable and raved about it to his friends. His Internet service was fast and he was ecstatic. He showed it off to his peers and urged them to sign up. He became a one-man booster for the cable modem. Then he noticed that the connection was getting slower and slower. Over time, his Internet connection became so slow, especially at peak times, that it didn't seem much faster than his old dial-up modem.

Soon he was e-mailing everyone in his address book. His message? Forget cable modems. They are worthless.

If anyone he even barely knew mentioned the cable modem, he would launch into his horror story. He canceled his service and is unlikely to sign up again, he says, even if the cable company added more capacity and guaranteed a fast connection speed. He felt so betrayed by the cable company that he even looked into switching his cable television service to satellite.

The cable company lost a highly involved customer, probably for life, and also the friends he convinced about the bad service, those in the future he would have persuaded to buy the service, and others whom his friends told, and so on. All that short-term market-share gain turned into a much larger missed opportunity. This is far from an isolated case. The trade journals, websites, and online journals are full of stories like this one.

The phone companies are making similar market-share-inspired blunders with their DSL business. "They're putting up so many lines just to get market share," Nick Rigas, a consultant at Atlantic-ACM, a telecom strategy and research outfit, told *USA Today*. "They're nowhere close to being where they need to be to provide the quality service that people expect."

Even well-connected customers are getting the shaft instead of service. Tom Wolzien, an analyst at the influential telecom consulting firm known as Sanford C. Bernstein Inc., ordered DSL service for his suburban New York home. Installation delays became so pronounced that he began keeping a diary. Soon he began sending his diary to his corporate clients and institutional investors—after all, it was a good on-the-ground account of the DSL business, which increasingly didn't live up to the rosy image offered by phone company executives. Eventually, the CEO of Verizon—Mr. Wolzien's DSL provider—read his tale of wasted time, bureaucratic hassle, and growing delays. But even the Verizon CEO couldn't set things straight. It took 111 days for Mr. Wolzien to get DSL service installed in his Westchester County, New York, home.

Many more "civilians"—ordinary customers without access to industry leaders—have waited much longer. More than 50 percent of all DSL customers in America reported troublesome installations and were unhappy with customer service, according to a survey by *DSL Reports,* an online trade journal.

Outside America, phone operators are busy chasing market share and making the same mistakes. Skynet, in conjunction with Belgacom, a Belgian telecom, offered free installation as a promotion to sign up new customers for DSL in Brussels. They signed up so many new customers that existing customers, and those recently signed up, had trouble getting any DSL connection off and on for almost a month. Forget speed problems—customers couldn't even access their e-mail for a while. Customer anger mounted.

DSL companies had better hope that all of that market share was worth a parade of angry customers. Meanwhile, DSL providers have harmed their most important asset—a loyal and happy base of customers. So much for the pursuit of market share.

In fact, better customer care is often the key to low-share businesses' beating their larger rivals. This is true even in low-margin, so-called hostile industries.

The grocery business is one of the toughest in America, especially for the mom-and-pop independents.

The number of independently owned grocery stores in the United States plummeted 40 percent between 1988 and 1998—while the number of chain supermarkets climbed 16 percent.

This is a highly competitive business where scale appears to have real advantages—bulk purchases, efficient central warehouses, greater selection, and so on.

Yet a recent Food Marketing Institute Study—the Washington-based group is funded by both chain supermarkets and independents—found that many of the smaller stores are thriving. Their secret? They follow a strategy completely opposite that of market-share-minded DSL providers. The independent grocers focus on customer service.

"Size is not the issue," Karen Brown, a Food Marketing Institute senior vice president, told the press. "The grocery business is customer driven, so you can be successful regardless of your size if you know who your customers are and make sure you supply the products and services they want."

Take D&P Foods of Flasher, North Dakota, a town of 300 people fifty miles from the state capital of Bismarck. Owner Dennis Hatzenbuhler told Office.com that he has reinvented the concept of the supermarket. He takes orders by phone, makes deliveries to local customers' homes, and has been known to drive 100 miles round trip to get special items for customers. Of course, he charges more. His customers "are willing to pay extra for the convenience," he says.

Or consider G. Ferrari Foods Inc., a family-owned store in San Francisco. The store targets "foodies," highly involved customers who want the latest and the best. So G. Ferrari Foods has obscure cheeses flown in from Italy and a much larger selection of olive oil than its rivals. It is a story of big margins and happy customers.

THE BOTTOM LINE

Companies do an astonishing array of self-destructive, counterintuitive, and downright strange things to boost market share. Some don't see any real alternative. The CEO of one of the world's largest operators of wireless telephone networks just looks across the restaurant table at me: "What else can I do?"

That is the fundamental question: What is the proven alternative to market-share madness? Turn the page and find out.

CHAPTER FIVE

Dinosaurs Were Big, Too: Why Profit Leaders Beat Market Leaders

There are three types of companies in every line of business: the ones that make the most money (the profit leaders), the ones that have the largest share of the market (the market leaders), and everyone else.

Sometimes the profit leaders are also market leaders—years of superior profitability have given them the ability to expand profitably. Profit leaders do become market leaders fairly regularly, but rarely does a market leader become a profit leader. More often, the profit leaders are not the biggest in the industry and, sometimes, not even the second biggest.

Let's sharpen our terms. A profit leader is a firm that earns the highest rate of return in its line of business, as defined by standard industry classification, or SIC, codes. A market leader is the firm with the largest share of sales in that same line of business.

If you want to be a profit leader, this chapter provides a road map, showing how leaders in diverse businesses have resisted the blandishments of market-share mania and created businesses that lead their industry in profits. They have avoided the dangerous discounts that sap the strength of brands, avoided foolish mergers, and focused on the customer—not the competition. They maintained or increased margins, while continuously cutting costs. Sometimes they perfected business models designed by others; sometimes they clung tenaciously to their original vision; and sometimes they set off on the road to profit leadership after putting on the brakes to years of bad business decisions.

That leaves two important interrelated questions: What do profit leaders have in common? And how does a company become a profit leader?

In this chapter, we examine three profit leaders: Dell (also a market leader), Ryanair (a profit leader in a growing market), and Hoffman-LaRoche's medical testing division (a profit leader in a mature market). Several important lessons—which extend far beyond the boundaries of their respective businesses—will emerge. But one important constant should be clear from the beginning: These businesses are not trying to grow into profitability, they grow profitably.

Case Study: Hoffman-LaRoche

For a long time, F. Hoffman-LaRoche's medical testing division wasn't a leader in any sense. It wasn't the biggest, it wasn't the best, and it certainly wasn't the most profitable. Roche Diagnostics Systems, as the division was known, was a perennial also-ran, a softly ridiculed division left in the dust by more innovative and more aggressive rivals.

The division focused on blood cultures, chemistry instruments for labs, drug-testing kits, and pregnancy tests. Other products monitored tumors and provided chemicals for drug testing in prisons and jails. It also sells testing products and services to "doctors, researchers, patients, hospitals and laboratories worldwide," according to company reports. It sells everything from tiny strips for testing the blood of diabetics to massive DNA-testing machines. It was no one's idea of a growth business.

By 2001, the medical testing division was one of the most profitable in its parent company's portfolio. It was also the profit leader in its line of business. By 2001, it became the largest supplier of diagnostic health care products in the world. U.S. sales alone exceeded $1 billion. How did they do this?

In 1990, the ailing division got an aggressive new leader, Jean-Luc Belingard. He took a hard look at the sprawling global division and discovered that it was a laggard in every one of its primary markets: France, Italy, Japan, and the United States. There were a few bright points in the United States—the division did well in workplace drug testing and in testing convicts. But these were hardly growth markets in the early 1990s and weren't particularly high-margin gambits, to boot.

Looking at the big picture, Mr. Belingard saw an unfocused organization that lurched from market to market, searching for growth. And the division's energy was thinly spread over a large area—the unit was in so many segments that it was regarded as a specialist in none. No single market—except perhaps the U.S. law enforcement officers involved in drug testing—had a clear idea of what Roche Diagnostics did.

Since its founding in 1969 the division had tried to differentiate itself based on the strength of its research and technical innovations. This is a typical failing of "science-based companies"—what matters most to the scientists and executives simply does not matter to customers. Maybe it could matter to customers if those values were communicated with clear benefits, such as "Our world-class research means fewer testing errors—and fewer headaches for you—than the competition's tests." But the division had never gone down that road.

Then Mr. Belingard made a vital and important decision. He wasn't going to do what everyone expected, at least not right away. He didn't overhaul the division's vast product offerings and he didn't spend millions on a new marketing strategy. And, most important, he didn't set out targets of market-share growth.

He knew that the most effective way to change a division was with a simple message: Let's differentiate based on customer service, not research and innovation. After all, the benefits are clearer to customers and easier to explain to employees. (For our purposes, it is worth noting that he implicitly considered market-share growth an ancillary benefit, not a target.)

Of course, every company likes to think that it has good customer service. (Still, how many CEOs dare to call their own 800 number and find out?)

What sets Roche Diagnostics apart is the sophisticated approach they took to customer service—and the thorough, methodical way they went about providing truly excellent customer care. (In this account, I am greatly indebted to a research paper entitled "Customer Delight and the Bottom Line" by Timothy L. Keiningham, Melinda K. M. Goddard, Terry G. Vavra, and Andrew J. Iaci. I heartily recommend reading their work in the October 1999 edition of *Marketing Management* and elsewhere.)

Too many companies settle for "customer satisfaction." The buyer gets what he expects, at a price he considers reasonable. Have a research company phone him up and chances are he'll say: "Yup, I'm satisfied." He's content. The product or service is good enough. He's buying it, isn't he?

Yet some brands attract and retain customers who are more than satisfied. Marketing experts call this magical state "customer delight." Roche Diagnostics wasn't the first firm to focus on customer delight.[1]

Xerox Corp., which has also adapted a version of customer delight, found that totally satisfied customers were six times more likely to repurchase the firm's products over the next eighteen months than customers who said they were simply satisfied.[2]

Customer delight seems to translate into more repeat business and greater word of mouth in favor of a company's products or services, and a greater "share of wallet"—what the customer spends in a category—goes to the favored company. In short, customer delight is the way customers form an emotional attachment to your company and generate more sales.

A delighted customer is someone whose expectations are exceeded. Delighted customers often say they are "pleasantly surprised" when they try a product or service for the first time. And every sale gives them the same pleasurable experience.

But how do you promote and measure customer

delight? In a moment, we will see how Roche did it. But the short answer is that many customer satisfaction surveys ask buyers if they are satisfied and to rate that satisfaction on a scale of one to five. The people who write "five" are your delighted customers. But why do they? Do you know? Roche Diagnostics, which initially had very few delighted customers, didn't.

So Mr. Belingard vowed to make Roche Diagnostics into an engine of customer delight.

But announcing changes in the boardroom is easier than changing reality on the ground. Here's how Roche Diagnostics made its long march into the ranks of profit leaders:

Change the Management. Mr. Belingard created a new position at corporate headquarters called "head of global service quality and satisfaction." He appointed Robert-Denis Moulloud. And he put a new man, Carlo Medici, in charge of U.S. operations. (In 1999, Martin D. Madaus took charge of U.S. operations, in Indianapolis.)

If you want to change the way things work, you have to change the people in charge. Veterans may have all sorts of institutional knowledge, but too often they are wedded to the old ways. Any change is seen as an implicit criticism of their past performance, so they will usually fight it as politely as they can. New managers are more likely to be loyal to the executive who hired them. And they are more likely to implement his vision. Mr. Belingard simply didn't bring in executives whom he had worked with in other assignments; he chose leaders who were passionate about "customer delight."

Simply changing the managers is not enough. Leave the same incentives in place, and the new people will act like the old ones. But changing the focus is a crucial first step to changing the organization.

Announce the Strategy. At his first management meeting in the United States, Mr. Medici, the new head of American operations, declared that he planned to achieve "leadership and profitability through customer satisfaction."[3] He wanted the doctors, prison officials, and others who used Roche Diagnostics products to be delighted with its offerings. He kept his strategy simple and clear. It is vital to establish the goal and not simply hope that managers will "figure it out."

Measure, Measure, Measure. Incredibly, the American unit had never comprehensively gauged customer satisfaction. Mr. Moulloud and Mr. Medici changed that. For a time, they stumbled around: conducting focus groups with customers, hiring consultants, and retaining firms to conduct hour-long phone interviews with customers. While costly and time consuming, Roche executives were finally getting a brutally accurate picture of what their customers thought of them. The short answer? Not much.

Identify Moments of Truth. All of that customer research pointed to specific negative interactions between customers and the service staff. These became known internally as "moments of truth"[4]—points in the sales or service transaction when the customer learned just how much the firm cared about his needs.

The truth was, customer service was a mess. Phone the 800 number, and you'd get an automated system (press one for this, two for that). Once you escaped the electronic dungeon and actually reached a human being, chances were she would transfer you or take a message for someone else to phone you back. It wasn't her fault. Customer service was divided into a bevy of fiefdoms with rigidly defined missions. And she wasn't trained to answer your questions anyway. Even if she knew the answer, she would probably get in trouble for exceeding her authority. Roche Diagnostics has become a company where actual customer service was considered "risky."

So agents stuck to the rule book. Call with a simple question and the agent would page a field engineer who promised to call back within twenty-four hours. This wasn't customer delight, it was more like customer torture.

Benchmarks. Detailed and rigorous customer service surveys illustrated the problem. Roche hired Coopers & Lybrand (now PriceWaterhouseCoopers), which analyzed and compared Roche's practices with its rivals. "There were many metrics [out of 70] on which Roche fell short for industry practice and on which Roche customers gave particularly low satisfaction ratings,"[5] according to *Marketing Management,* a trade journal.

But denial is more than a river in Egypt. "The water cooler question became 'Aren't all customers hard to please?' followed by the reassuring refrain 'Maybe we aren't so bad after all.'"[6] Resistance was welling up among experienced managers.

Benchmarking became critical to defusing internal resistance. Research showed that customers ranked competitors higher in a number of key areas. Now top management had an objective answer to its homegrown critics. Now there was an objective reason to change.

Usually benchmarking is a way to ensure that a company is no worse, and maybe slightly better, than its direct competitors. It does not translate into a strategic advantage because it is not a real point of differentiation. No one wins business simply because they meet the "industry standard."

However, benchmarking can be an effective way to nullify or reduce a rival's perceived strength. Roche used its benchmarking efforts to overcome internal resistance and to ensure that the division's strategy was implemented. Few companies even recognize the problem of internal resistance.

Take Action. Mr. Medici set up a "benchmarking task force" to improve performance. The task force used a kind of triage to select its goals. They took on the worst first, then went after the comparably easier ones, and finally, with the wind of success at their back, went after the merely difficult ones. With each improvement, the same customer survey was used—in order to have constant feedback on their efforts. The steady improvements built up momentum to continue their efforts.

These hard-won improvements meant that entire departments had to be redesigned. Roche's six service fiefdoms were better integrated and personnel were cross-trained. Now a customer service agent can answer simple technical questions, reorder a product, and provide basic product information. The number of call transfers—almost half of all calls in some months—was dramatically reduced. Today very few calls are transferred and all transfers are to human beings, not answering machines.

Some misleading internal measurements were dropped: One metric assessed quality by the amount of time it took for a "medical technologist" to phone back a customer who had left a message. But this was useless. The customer didn't care how long it took to have her call returned—she wanted an answer now. This internal measurement was dropped.

And, of course, the automated phone system was scrapped during business hours. When these misleading metrics—and the incentives that went with them—were changed, performance improved and so did customer satisfaction.

The result: increased profit. It all paid off. Today Roche Diagnostics is one of the fastest-growing firms in its line of business and is the fastest-growing division in F. Hoffmann-LaRoche's global health care group. While it still doesn't have the largest market share in its business, it does make the most money. Roche Diagnostics, welcome to the profit leaders.

Case Study: Dell Computer Corp.

Dell is both a market leader and a profit leader.

Dell has a long record of growing faster than its markets. Take the first quarter of 2001: Total global shipments of personal computers rose to 31.6 million, a gain of 852,000. Dell's shipment surged by 957,000 units. And this was during a downturn in worldwide sales.

What about profits? Dell was the only one of the top six American personal computer makers to report a profit in the first quarter of 2001. While it reported the first drop in profit margins since 1993, let's keep this in perspective. Dell is making money while its rivals, Compaq Computer Corp. and Hewlett-Packard Co. (which plan to merge) announced write-downs of $450 million and $100 million, respectively. Overall, Dell is pretty healthy, in an industry characterized by price wars, layoffs, and relentless technological change.

And, by most accounts, Dell is the leader in market share. Dell now owns roughly 25 percent of U.S. personal computer sales, up from 6.8 percent in 1996, according to International Data Corp., a Framingham, Massachusetts–based research organization. Dell has the largest market share in worldwide personal computer sales, at 13.1 percent. Dell's growth in market share is almost entirely at the expense of its competitors. Dell now holds 95 percent of the desktop computer market for corporations, according to *Barron's*. Dell's stock climbed an incredible 86,900 percent from 1990 to 2000. While Dell is off of its peak—like most high-tech issues—it is clearly rebounding while its competitors' stocks test new lows. "It may not be making a fortune, but it is making money while others lose it," writes Jay Palmer, a *Barron's* reporter.[7]

If you talk to Dell executives, you will hear a lot about market-share growth. But don't be fooled. Dell doesn't set market-share targets and then slash prices or use cheaper components to get it. Instead, Dell has long stuck to three key strategic decisions and reaped the benefits:

- Fanatic cost control through supply-chain management
- Control of a strategic sales channel
- Deep and broad knowledge of its customers and excellent market intelligence

Cost Control. Dell is single-minded about constantly paring its costs. Sometimes this emphasis on cost cutting goes to amusing extremes, according to the *Wall Street Journal.* Company founder Michael S. Dell once noticed that a supplier had provided cinnamon rolls for a meeting of senior managers. "Take those back and let's knock the price off the next shipment of materials you bring," Mr. Dell declared. "We don't need food. We want a better price."[8]

It might sound absurd, but no one is in the dark about the chief executive's commitment to cost control.

Indeed, Dell's strategy is built around cost containment. "Contrary to what most companies say, it's not necessary to be price competitive," says James T. Vanderslice, Dell's copresident. "It's most necessary to be cost-competitive."[9] Translation: Though it is extremely competitive on price, Dell's managers know that a sustainable price advantage is built on a stable cost advantage.

How do you build a significant cost advantage? Dell did it with low staff costs, innovative supply-chain management techniques, and harnessing the power of software to streamline the production process.

Human overhead amounts to only 11.5 cents per dollar of sales, well below Gateway Inc.'s staff costs of 16 cents per sales dollar, 21 cents at Compaq, and 22.5 cents at Hewlett-Packard.[10] And those figures were compiled before 1,700 layoffs, announced in the spring of 2001.

Dell uses contract workers, where possible. That gives the computer maker the power and flexibility to increase or decrease production without having to maintain a costly, fixed labor pool. That gives Dell the freedom to balance the size of its workforce with the size of its sales volume.

Also, managers have the ability to redefine jobs in order to boost productivity—an indirect way of cutting costs.

But the real cost savings are in materials, not people. The costs of parts and other materials account for almost 75 percent of Dell's total revenues. Dell paid some $21 billion to suppliers in 2000. "Shaving 0.1% off [that] can have a bigger impact than, say, improving manufacturing productivity by 10%," Dick L. Hunter, Dell's vice president in charge of supply chain management, told *BusinessWeek.*[11]

Dell shaves supply costs by forging an unusually close relationship with its vendors. That is easier for Dell than for other companies its size, because the computer maker has relatively few suppliers. Only thirty vendors account for 75 percent of its purchases by dollar value and only fifty firms account for 95 percent of its purchases.[12] Dell's managers are in contact with many of those vendors on a daily basis.

No one in the industry seems as tightly interwoven with its supply chain as Dell. Dell sends those vendors weekly sales forecasts, so they had better plan their production runs and, of course, cut costs. Dell negotiates hard to make sure that it—and ultimately its customers—realize some of those savings.

Few companies share sales forecasts with their vendors on a monthly or even quarterly basis. Some don't even share their numbers at all. Maybe they are afraid it will empower their suppliers to demand better terms. But it seems to work wonders for Dell.

About those contracts that Dell signs with parts providers: Most are keyed to changes in the suppliers' costs. So when costs fall—as they do fairly steadily in this sector—Dell reaps lower prices while vendors maintain their margins. This helps Dell maintain its cost advantage while its rivals are often locked into long-term contracts.

As for the handful of long-term contracts that Dell does sign, the computer maker is not above quickly renegotiating the terms when prices move suddenly. One price spike and Dell's executives are on the phone.

How can Dell react so quickly? It has a dedicated in-house cost-control team, which watches up-to-the-minute results from suppliers' production lines all the way to Dell's factory floor. This tracking information is online and can be accessed by any Dell leader anywhere in the world. Key personnel receive an e-mail alert as soon as costs climb or sink suddenly.

In short, Dell has created a "virtual merger" with all of its key suppliers. Information is rapidly shared—and moves both ways—between suppliers and Dell's assembly plants. It is as if its vendors have an office down the hall and can be quickly called in to address emerging problems. You could call it "supply chain Nirvana"—a seamless ribbon that binds together everyone who puts something into a Dell computer. Or, as Dell's Mr. Hunter puts it: "Our goal is to replace inventory with information."[13]

How can inventory replace information? Let's answer that question in a roundabout way. Companies maintain large inventories as a hedge against bad information. If you are making machine tools, you probably need a backlog of steel because you don't know how quickly you can get more or at what price. And if you guess wrong, and have too little, you have a factory of expensive machinery sitting idle. You're paying the overhead (labor costs, debt service, the cost of missed production, and so on) and getting nothing in return. What if you guess wrong and stock up on too many raw materials? You've just tied up a lot of capital in useless metal, which eats up precious warehouse space, and rusts.

So, in the 1970s economy, a good inventory control manager was worth his weight in gold.

"Just-in-time" inventory management practices were supposed to take a lot of the risk and cost out of this game. And it did. Inventories and costs fell as managers learned to use computers to better plan their inventory needs and their production plans.

But the three important drivers in the inventory game still lay outside of managers' control: sales, prices from suppliers, and suppliers' ability to produce it. All sorts of elaborate computer models were supposed to predict these things, but, like weather forecasts, they were too often wrong.

The problem was that all the necessary information existed outside the four walls of the firm. Dell solved the problems of sales, supply costs, and shipment time brilliantly.

Control of a Strategic Sales Channel. First Dell was built on a direct sales model—the buyers contact Dell directly and agree on the price and features they want. This takes a lot of the guesswork out of sales forecasting—simply because Dell gets the order before it makes the product. But it doesn't take *all* of the guesswork out; a lot of planning is needed to make computers to order. Over the years, Dell has developed a lot of market intelligence through its direct contact with buyers—it talks to some 10,000 business customers in its main PC market every day. Those orders, when aggregated into millions, allows Dell to see patterns and anticipate sales. It doesn't mean that Dell is always right—sales forecasting can be an unruly beast—but thanks to its direct sales channel, the cost of being wrong about future sales is much less costly.

Now let's look at supply costs and shipment time—the other big question marks in inventory management. Until recently, what it cost your supplier to make something and how long it took him to make it were closely guarded secrets. The psychology was a bit like that of cold war spies: If the "enemy" finds out, he will use this vital information to his advantage. He might hammer down prices or decide to take his business to another outfit that can deliver more quickly. So it's best to keep the buyer in the dark.

But keeping buyers in the dark meant that the purchaser had to maintain a large and costly inventory. (That might not seem so bad, because it means that you've just sold him more stuff than he really needs.) But, of course, your suppliers are doing the same thing to you (ouch!) and your buyer isn't telling you about his future plans, for the same kind of reasoning. So the business landscape was shrouded in secrecy, distrust, and excess costs.

Dell practices a form of "open book management" with suppliers. Dell shares detailed sales forecasts and hourly production estimates while suppliers reveal their costs and margins and delivery times. So inventories can be a lot leaner at both ends of the supply chain. By sucking some of the risk out of the process, Dell and its suppliers enjoy lower costs. And that gives Dell a sustainable cost advantage over its rivals.

Dell maintains only a five-day inventory of parts at all of its plants. Its rivals in the personal computer market maintain thirty-day or even forty-five-day inventories. In the data storage market, Dell also maintains a five-day inventory, compared with a ninety-one-day inventory at market leader EMC.[14] Dell executives have repeatedly told the press that they plan to cut inventories to two days' worth of production.

Lean inventories quickly turn into cost advantages in this industry. In the computer building business, component costs drop an average of 1 percent per week. "So if a competitor has four weeks' worth of inventory and we have one week's, right there we have 3% worth of material costs advantage. That can mean a 2% to 3% advantage to the bottom line," Mr. Hunter says.[15]

Which brings us to: How do they do it? Dell and its suppliers share an intranet program developed by i2 Technologies. Using a complex algorithm, the computer program is able to find the most efficient way to schedule production runs. As a result, Dell and many of its suppliers now break their production runs down into two-hour cycles. They can quickly retime production lines if demand drops or part prices rise. That means higher productivity, fewer overtime hours, less overproduction, and more efficient manufacturing operations. Thanks to the new software, Dell could run its assembly operations with only six hours' worth of inventory on hand.

Other software packages help Dell minimize unused or outdated inventory. This inventory deadweight amounts to 0.1 to 0.5 percent of Dell's material costs in any given year. Some direct competitors write off as much as 3 percent of material costs as deadweight inventory. As a result, Dell wastes less and saves more money.

How? When Dell managers sense slackening demand—fewer orders for particular components—they set off a threshold, say, 20,000 more units and no more. Usually that threshold is set by calculating Dell's small inventory on hand and modeling anticipatory future sales. Once that threshold is announced, the limit is set in stone.

Dell actually addresses some of its supply issues in its sales operations. Say a plant is anticipating shortage of a particular part in the next few hours. If managers can get the components quickly—on one of their hourly shipments—fine. If not, they will try to use an alternative vendor. If that vendor also can't deliver in time, a Dell supply manager contacts his opposite number in sales and marketing. Together, they make certain decisions very quickly—either increase lead times for customers wanting that component (which usually shifts demand to other parts) or change prices on comparable items. If you e-mail Dell and find that flat-panel displays are suddenly cheaper, perhaps they are having problems getting certain monitors.

These prices can change very quickly because all of Dell's prices are online. A *Wall Street Journal* reporter recently discovered that a certain personal computer was listed at $50 cheaper than the advertised price in the *New York Times* on *the same day* he phoned in. Thus, Dell keeps supply and demand in balance and keeps its production lines humming.

Dell's salespeople have the freedom to set prices, within a range set by regional managers. That gives them the flexibility to call on a company and match almost any price the competition is offering. What about prices below the regional targets? Dell maintains a hotline for sales staff who need a "special price" to close the deal. Headquarters gives the salesman an answer within one hour. But this isn't buying market share—every sale is profitable.

These operational efficiencies—its constant focus on costs—allow Dell to ruthlessly lower prices, while earning healthy returns. That's what makes Dell both a profit leader and a market leader.

Case Study: Ryanair

Think of a wildly successful airline that makes money when its rivals grimly report losses, run by a devil-take-the-hindmost CEO who lists his hobbies as "smoking, drinking, and chasing loose women."[16] The airline has a reputation for wacky stunts, cheap tickets, and explosive growth. *The Economist* magazine calls it "the most profitable airline in the world." The *Wall Street Journal* calls it "one of the world's hottest airline stocks."[17]

Wanna bet that you are thinking of Southwest Airlines?

Sure, Southwest fits almost all of the criteria. Southwest stock—under the cheeky name LUV—has increased more than 2,000 percent since 1980. It has the lowest costs of any major U.S. carrier and its legendary CEO, Herb Kelleher, who stepped down in June 2001, has a reputation for chain-smoking, drinking copious amounts of Wild Turkey, and delivering solid, sustained growth in a notoriously cyclical industry. Southwest has never had an unprofitable quarter since becoming a publicly traded company, and it has never laid anyone off—ever. Southwest definitely qualifies as a profit leader in the U.S. air travel market.

But we are not talking about Southwest.

Ryanair is the carrier that has the largest profit margin of any major airline in the world per passenger-mile traveled. It is also one of the fastest growing. And it succeeded by perfecting Southwest's flight plan.

Ryanair is Europe's largest low-fare airline—it is the Continent's answer to America's Southwest. Indeed, the Dublin-based carrier expressly modeled itself on the

Dallas-based airline (but it is not owned by Southwest). Like the Japanese automakers who first studied Detroit and then outperformed it, Ryanair has exceeded Southwest's exceptional performance in many key areas. The star pupil could teach his master a few tricks.

While Ryanair is the market leader in the nascent discount airfare segment in the European market, it has less than 1 percent of the total European air travel market (Southwest holds about 5 percent of the U.S. air travel market, but the discount travel market is larger, older, and more established in the United States). "Ryanair's earnings growth and return on capital are higher than Southwest's," notes a recent Morgan Stanley Dean Witter analyst's report.

Still, Ryanair's results belie its relatively small size. Its profit margin is in excess of 20 percent—well above Southwest's excellent average profit margin of 15.5 percent. (The European airline average is 6.6 percent.) Its rapid growth—what one analyst calls "vertical liftoff"—reminds one of Southwest's early days. Ryanair carried less than one million passengers in 1990; it carried nine million in 2001. Most interestingly, its costs are probably the lowest in the world. Consider "cost per available seat mile," a standard industry measure. Ryanair's costs are 30 percent below the European industry average, while the number of passengers transported per employee is 40 percent higher. Thus, Ryanair can make money when its planes are a little over half-full, while its rivals need their planes to be three-quarters full before breaking even. (Ryanair's planes are on average more than 75 percent full.)

Unlike Southwest, Ryanair was not a success from the beginning. Southwest began in a San Antonio bar and made money with its first flights.

Ryanair hit turbulence soon after its 1985 takeoff and was in a downward spiral by 1989, when airline founder Tony Ryan sat down with his financial adviser, Michael O'Leary. Mr. O'Leary looked over the books. He saw that Ryanair had had five chief executives in five years, lost nearly $25 million, and operated an extensive network of money-losing routes. The young Mr. O'Leary didn't mince words: "Shut the bloody thing down!" he advised.[18]

Instead, Mr. Ryan had a different idea. He persuaded Mr. O'Leary to go see an "old friend" in Dallas. At the Palm Steakhouse, Mr. O'Leary met Herb Kelleher, then Southwest's CEO. After a few drinks, Mr. O'Leary became convinced that Mr. Kelleher was a "genius."

He agreed to serve as Ryanair's interim CEO and adopt Southwest's business model. For his pains, Mr. O'Leary asked for, and got, 25 percent of Ryanair's future profits. Not bad for a guy with no experience in the airlines business. (Mr. O'Leary's take has since been scaled back, but it was still estimated at more than $30 million as of 2001.)

Mr. O'Leary didn't waste time. He quickly pruned away the unprofitable routes and got rid of the turboprop aircraft. Like Southwest, Ryanair decided to fly a single type of plane—the Boeing 737. That would save on spare parts, maintenance crews, and make each plane inter-changeable. Like Southwest, Ryanair flies into cheaper, secondary airports—which translates into lower handling charges, quicker turnaround times, and fewer flight delays. (Smaller airports have much less congestion; with only two dozen flights per day, there's no need for endless "holding patterns" or "stacked" aircraft.) And Ryanair is definitely low-frills—unlike Southwest it doesn't even offer its passengers free peanuts or ice. (Eliminating ice saved the carrier $50,000 per year.) Sandwiches and drinks are sold the way full-service international airlines hawk duty-free goods—in the aisles, for cash.

Plane crews are paid productivity bonuses and many are shareholders—which connects worker sentiment with financial incentives. So they don't resist doing more than one job at once. Flight attendants clean and restock the planes, not costly ground crews.

Mr. O'Leary made other changes. The business class section was abolished. The fare structure was simplified: 70 percent of all seats were now sold for one of the two lowest prices. Ryanair reported its first profit in 1991 and hasn't lost money since. By 1994, it was the biggest carrier on the Dublin-London route. It still is.

So far, Ryanair has been following Southwest's business model to a T. But three things set Ryanair apart—and hold important lessons for enterprises far afield from the hypercompetitive airline sector:

- Customer advocacy
- Cost control
- Channel control

Customer Advocacy. Everyone is in the customer service business, but Ryanair takes it to a different level.

Consider Ryanair's customer segment: budget conscious, relatively young people who are interested in getting from point A to point B—as opposed to higher-income, older people who want to "travel."

Ryanair gets their attention with tickets to the south of France from London for $30. In fact, this is one of Ryanair's *higher* fares. More than one million passengers

in 2000 traveled for less than $10. That is not a misprint—
the taxi to the airport usually costs more than a flight on
Ryanair. (We will look at how they can make hefty profits from these crazy fares in the next section.)

What's important is what Ryanair tells its customers,
after it has their attention. It tells them in a hundred
different ways that the airline is "on their side." Call it
"outlandish customer advocacy." Virtually all of its com-
munications with the public—everything from billboards
to press releases to saucy quotes in newspapers—pokes
fun at its competitors' high prices.

Their message is aggressive, even mean—but it
seems to resonate with their customers. Ryanair consistently takes the side of budget travelers against higher airport landing fees, costly foreign exchange fees, and
ever-high airport car-parking charges. The power of this
message is best shown by example:

- Ryanair ran ads in British newspapers attacking British
  Airways. The headline? "Expensive BA . . . ds!" Of
  course, British Airways, known locally as BA (hence
  the play on words), sued Ryanair. When the airline lost,
  Ryanair triumphantly issued a press release: "BA are
  expensive and the High Court says so."

- When Air France ended its Glasgow to Paris route,
  Ryanair's sales manager for Scotland, Kathryn Munro,
  told the press: "Au revoir, Air France! Even France's
  government-subsidized airline cannot compete with
  Ryanair on price or frequency—that's a huge embarrass-
  ment for them and leaves Ryanair as the only nonstop
  between Glasgow and Paris." Note the advertisement in
  the midst of the barbed reference to the competition?

Nor did Ms. Munro stop there. "And BA must be similarly red-faced. Incredibly, their Glasgow-Paris passengers are now being routed through Birmingham, adding at least another hour to the flight time. And, unbelievably, they're also being asked to pay up to £480 for the privilege of hanging around Birmingham Airport!"

It might be startlingly rude and self-serving, but it generates a lot of free media attention.

• Ryanair ran ads in Belgium to announce its new service from Charleroi, thirty miles south of Brussels. It deliberately poked the dominant Belgian airline in the eye. Beside a famous Brussels statue of a pissing boy, the ad (in French and Flemish) asked: "Pissed off by Sabena's high fares?"

When the Belgian carrier politely asked Ryanair to pull the ads, Ryanair's CEO Michael O'Leary wrote back an insulting letter attacking the carrier's high ticket prices. Naturally, this letter was translated into all of Belgium's official languages and sent to every newspaper in the country. Sabena later went out of business and Ryanair expanded into the German air market.

The point here is not that corporations should belittle and vex their rivals just to get some free ink. Far from it. What is important here is that Ryanair has forged a strong identity of fighting on behalf of customers. Ryanair's own unscientific polls show its customers overwhelmingly favor this kind of bluster, which is usually given with a friendly twinkle in the eye.

Ryanair's executives intuitively know that these travelers don't mind a bit of outlandish advertising. And that's what Ryanair delivers. And, of course, Ryanair's executives enjoy doing it. This kind of blarney has become part of the corporate culture. It's the kind of airline where the Dublin baggage handlers play a weekly soccer game with senior managers (including the CEO) every week. When a Ryanair air steward was selected to appear on Britain's *Big Brother* television series—one of those awful reality shows in which a group of people are sequestered in a house—Ryanair didn't miss a marketing opportunity, or a chance to reinforce its unique corporate culture. "All 1500 of us at Ryanair are rooting for Brian [Dowling], though he'd better get his kit [clothes] off soon, otherwise we'll send him a warning for under-exposure."

Ryanair is Europe's eighth largest airline—but none of the other major carriers would ever talk to the press this way. But its unique corporate culture gives it the freedom to mount such unorthodox media campaigns. Ryanair's CEO told me that tweaking competitors is "the most fun you can have with your clothes on."

In short, what Ryanair has done is create a brand identity that extends beyond low prices. Ryanair talks about its competitors the way their passengers might talk in a pub—and that gives the message a kind of credibility with its target market. While Ryanair's strategy probably has not been tried by another company its size—though Southwest comes close—it probably should be.

Still, there is an important lesson here. Connect with customers in a credible and visceral way: Be seen as an advocate for your customers and employees—and don't get sued.

Cost Control. *All of the pranks aside, Ryanair is very serious about controlling costs. Single-minded, even. The only way to run a low-fare airline is to continually trim costs, something that Mr. O'Leary repeatedly stresses—albeit in more earthy terms.*

Aside from using Southwest's techniques, here is what makes Ryanair the lowest-cost carrier in the world on a per-mile-traveled basis:

- *Flat management.* "We keep the management structure extremely flat. As we grow, we're only adding aircraft, pilots, in-flight people and engineers. We don't need these layers of bureaucracy or layers of management," Mr. O'Leary told the *Wall Street Journal Europe.*[19]

  He's not kidding. The corporate headquarters is a small office at Dublin Airport. When I phone the CEO, I can usually get him on the phone in five minutes—unless he answers the phone himself. There are only eight senior managers at corporate headquarters.

- *Low staff levels.* The typical Ryanair flight has two "air hostesses"—compared with five on other carriers. Compare Ryanair with Aer Lingus, the former Irish monopoly airline. Ryanair carried 9 million passengers with 1,500 staff in 2001, while Aer Lingus carried 6 million with 7,000 employees.

- *Fast turnaround of planes.* Ryanair can unload, clean, restock, and reload a plane in twenty-five minutes—probably the fastest in the industry. That means Ryanair is able to make eight flights in six hours, as opposed to six flights by competing carriers. Post–September 11 security procedures have slowed turnaround times a bit, but it's still one of the fastest in the airline sector.

- *No extras.* There is no frequent flyer plan. Why pay for the extra computer system and give away "free flights"? The management team, including the CEO, takes turns managing the ground and baggage staff. Passengers are asked to take their sandwich wrappers and magazines with them. Oh, and don't bother looking for a company in-flight magazine—there isn't one.

  "In its no frills fervor, Ryanair even refuses to use those extendable boarding corridors at airports because it's quicker to park a plane at the gate, roll stairs up to the front and back doors and let passengers hustle across the tarmac," notes the *Wall Street Journal Europe.*[20]

- *Cheap, secondary airports.* Ryanair, like Southwest, negotiates extremely low-cost, long-term deals with secondary airports. Fees usually run only $1.50 per passenger over fifteen years, compared with an average rate of $22 per passenger at major airports. Some of these airports are at former U.S. military bases in Europe, including the Frankfurt-Hahn airport in Germany. These privatized airfields are desperate for air traffic and Ryanair is hungry for a deal.

  Airports, like Italy's Rimini, that raise rates either lose Ryanair's business or suffer a blistering attack in the press.

  Ryanair chooses its airports strategically. Its low-cost airport hub, outside of London, is now the second fastest growing airport of the world's 125 airports, according to Raymond James and Associates, a leading investment research firm.

- *Focus on profits.* Ryanair only opens new routes that the airline believes will be immediately profitable, unlike competing airlines, which want to expand into new markets and hope that the profits will catch up to their expansion plans. In other words, they focus on profits, not market share.

Overall, Ryanair is relentlessly looking to cut expenses—even though it has the best profit margins in the world. Ryanair's 32 percent cost advantage over other European carriers is even greater than Southwest's 25 percent cost advantage over U.S. carriers. Ryanair's cost per available seat mile—the metric used by the airline industry to track costs—is 11 cents, compared with almost 13 cents on British Airways, 16 cents on Air France, and 20 cents on SAS.[21] Morgan Stanley Dean Witter analysts estimate that Ryanair's costs per passenger are "among the lowest in the world."[22]

Some may suspect that all of this cost-cutting is a stealth plan to boost market share. Not exactly. Ryanair has no plans to raise prices, and, indeed, its fares have been falling for the past five years. Low fares are the basis of its business model, not a short-term strategy to woo customers and jack up prices.

Cost of Its Sales Channel. Ryanair recently launched Ryanair.com, a website for booking tickets and other travel-related services. This was not a belated effort to join the dot-com craze—but a sophisticated attempt to get control of its sales channel, its connection to the customer.

Let's step back and take a look at the direct cost of sales in the airline business. The bulk of ticket sales come through travel agents, who charge 5 percent to 7.5 percent commission. In the glory days of the 1970s, travel agents earned even larger commissions—but passenger traffic was less than one-quarter what it is today.

Central reservations systems—Galileo, Apollo, and so on—charge another 4.5 percent. And the cost of maintaining the airlines' own computerized reservations system—which talks to the central reservations systems by modem—costs another 1 percent of ticket sales.

All told, travel agents and reservations systems cost 13 percent of an airline's ticket price. That's a lot in a small-margin business.

Worse, it cuts the airline off from its customers. It is harder to predict future traffic flows—is the tourist season slumping or are travelers simply holding out for better deals? Also, through agents, it is harder to drive traffic with new fares. Often travel agents get a higher commission to put a passenger on a slightly more expensive competitor. So it becomes harder to react to quick moves in demand—the airline finds out long after the travel agents. So agents complicate the most complicated, but critical, part of the airline business—that is, managing the traffic flow so the planes are always as full as possible and never empty or oversubscribed.

Ryanair took control of its sales channel in two stages:

Stage One: After Lufthansa cut its commission to travel agents to 5 percent from 7.5 percent, Ryanair demanded the same terms. This is a delicate act—travel agents are generally the source of more than 60 percent of all ticket sales. A good relationship with them is critical to keeping an airline in the air, while lower costs are the key to keeping it in the black.

After winning that round, Ryanair gave its legally required notice to withdraw from several central reservations systems, including Galileo and Amadeus.

Stage Two: Meanwhile, Ryanair.com was in the works. The idea was to gradually shift airline bookings from agents to the website—which had no commission and no central reservations system.

Finally, Ryanair developed a new internal reservations system that was cheaper to maintain. The new system cost only 0.66 percent of ticket prices to run, compared with the older system's 1 percent overhead fee. The aim was to lower direct cost of ticket sales from 13 percent to 0.66 percent over three years.

To lure customers to book online, Ryanair offered a somewhat lower ticket price.

Then, Ryanair.com got swamped. Its cost-conscious customers were more than happy to book direct to save a few pence.

In 2000, more than 60 percent of ticket sales were through agents. By June 2001, that figure had dropped to 8 percent. Direct sales, through the Web and telephone, now account for 92 percent of Ryanair's bookings, according to company reports.

Overnight, Ryanair.com became the busiest travel site in Europe. At 50,000 bookings per week, Ryanair.com does more than double the number of transactions of travelocity.com. It even outpaces the sales of Amazon.co.uk—Amazon's British website, and one of Europe's busiest sites in any category.

This gives Ryanair a significant cost advantage. Other airlines have been slow to move into the direct sales channel. British Airways books only 2 percent of its tickets online. The major American carriers generated less than 10 percent of revenues online in 2001. Even mighty Southwest sells less than one-third of its tickets direct over the Web.

More important, control of the sales channel allows the carrier to offer discounts to shift passengers from full peak flights to less-full off-peak flights at the touch of a mouse.

The airline business is about capturing the "marginal passenger." Once fixed costs are covered, 90 percent of the fare of the extra airline passenger "would fall to the bottom line," notes a March 2000 analyst report by Merrion stockbrokers in Dublin.

Better still, the website could also be used to grow demand, not just capitalize it. Search engines will bring travelers to the site, even if the brand recognition of Ryanair isn't particularly high in their area.

Finally, the uniquely focused audience of the Web— thrifty travelers who know exactly where they want to go—offers opportunities for additional sales and advertising revenue. Ryanair.com has already added travel insurance and foreign exchange services.

THE BIG PICTURE

It's time to widen the frame and look at the big picture.

What do profit leaders have in common, besides strong growth and high profits?

No two businesses or profit leaders are exactly alike. There is no magic formula for being a profit leader. Still, certain common elements seem to connect many of them. With imagination and creativity, some of these common elements could be applied to any business.

Market-Share Ideology, Turned Upside Down. The old way of thinking was to win the biggest slice of market share and wait for the profits to roll in. From the stylish offices of the failed dot-coms to the grimy steel mills of western Pennsylvania, this model has failed to deliver. It's like "perfect competition," one of those chimera of economic theory that seems more often wrong than right.

Profit leaders turn this model upside down. They plan for profitable growth and let the market share come to them. It certainly works for Dell, Ryanair, Hoffman-LaRoche, and many others. And profit leaders usually avoid the mistakes we saw in Chapter Four: reckless discounts, mindless brand extensions, brand erosion, and pointless mergers.

A Democratic and Focused Corporate Culture. In many profit leaders, the corporate culture has been specifically designed to smash barriers between departments and flatten hierarchies. We're not talking about superficial moves like open-plan offices and dress-down Fridays.

A successful corporate culture is one where there are no barriers—where the central focus of the business trumps bureaucratic fiefdoms. Remember Hoffman-LaRoche's heroic efforts to eliminate the rigid divisions in customer service, Ryanair's unorthodox attempts—soccer matches between line workers and top managers, cheering on an employee who guest-stars on a hit television show—to keep barriers from building, and Dell's easy connections between its supply-chain managers and the sales and market division.

In most companies the chief executive can talk to whomever he wants and executives can address their peers in other units. In profit leaders, managers and even line employees communicate easily and directly with people in other divisions to solve common problems.

Financial incentives can play a role in overcoming corporate inertia. Increasing employee stock ownership and awarding productivity bonuses, as Dell and Ryanair do, is a good way to encourage employees to work together. One American Online manager tells me that she has AOL's stock price as a screen saver on her office computer. "When someone e-mails me about a problem, I think about that [number]," she says.

Cost Control. This is one of those humdrum but mission-critical tasks. Profit leaders do it extremely well.

Constant Innovation. Profit leaders recognize that competitive advantages are fleeting and require constant improvement. That means a continuous stream of new ideas and incremental improvements. Consider Dell's use of new i2 Technologies software to improve its production scheduling or Ryanair's website to sell more tickets at higher margins. Business leaders would do well to study Intel's 1985 move away from memory chips, where it was the market leader, to the more profitable market for processors. Without perpetual research and new ways of thinking about the business, that move would not have been possible. There would be no "Intel inside."

Customer Connection. Customers are the lifeblood of business and profit leaders think a lot about their bond with them.

- Hoffman-LaRoche used "customer delight" to create a crowd of customers who were pleased to re-order.

- Ryanair uses an aggressive form of customer advocacy.
- Dell uses its direct sales channel to constantly improve its market intelligence.

Channel Control. All three of the profit leaders that we examined used a version of the direct sales model. This has many advantages, but it is not the only way to control a sales channel.

McDonald's sells its products through franchises, but it networks them together to detect market shifts and tests new approaches through its storeowners.

Focus on Short-Term Profits. Loss leaders only lead to losses. Good luck trying to make up the profits later—competitors are rarely so obliging.

Ryanair never opens a route that doesn't promise to be immediately profitable. Dell sells its computers for low prices—but not at a loss.

Profit leaders usually focus on making money now. The future is another country.

Customer Selection. Profit leaders know who their customers are and focus on meeting their needs. It sounds simple, but it takes time and a lot of managerial energy. Profit leaders simply do this better than their rivals.

That means one must have a definable and defendable market niche. Gateway sells computers to everyone; Dell focuses on business buyers. That segment is defended by either a low-cost or high-service business model.

Coherence. The business models of most profit leaders—their corporate culture, their customer selection, their unique value proposition, their sustainable competitive advantage—usually fit together in a coherent, self-reinforcing way.

These enterprises are not split personalities—trying to present one face to customers, another to employees, still another to investors, and so on. Instead they are or try to be a seamless whole. They have been designed or redesigned to be who they are.

Vision and Management. To emulate the profit leaders takes a lot of thought, hard work, and concerted action. But it can be done. Even by the biggest companies. Once the goal of profitability is set, it is simply a question of vision and management.

What Dell, Ryanair, and Roche Diagnostics Systems have in common, at bottom, are managers who have a clear idea of where they want to go and how to get there—combined with the persistence necessary to overcome corporate inertia. Corporate inertia takes many forms and usually thrives through a constellation of constituencies, both internal and external (as discussed in Chapter Three). Dell and Roche strove to eliminate the barriers between departments and rewarded people for working toward a greater goal. Ryanair, which had the advantage of being a start-up, consciously created a corporate culture—with a lack of hierarchy or formality and a concentrated sense of purpose—that simply would not allow constituencies that threatened the health of the company to survive. (Of course, if and when Ryanair is double its present size, its corporate culture may change.)

And sometimes corporate inertia isn't simply resistance to change. Sometimes it's backed up by what looks like solid objections, which senior managers are too busy to fully consider. Roche took the time to do this—by countering a plausible, but wrong, belief that every customer is dissatisfied in some way and therefore can't be fully satisfied, with objective evidence to the contrary. Counterarguments should not be brushed aside or wished away—they need to be either addressed or admitted to.

And the biggest counterargument to the profit leader philosophy that I have scratched out is: Aren't we in an exceptional industry? Do those rules really apply to us? That is what the next chapter is about.

CHAPTER SIX

Networks and Double-Sided Markets: Why Microsoft and Visa Think About Market Share

Every rule has an exception—and everyone wants to believe that they are it. Their business is special and unique and therefore profits are not primary for them, but market share is. Too many managers believe that the myth of market share is not myth—for them. In a handful of cases, they're right: Market share is what matters.

In this chapter we examine the genuine special cases where market-share growth is essential and should be the aim of any sensible manager. We'll look at two massive enterprises—Microsoft and Visa—that prospered by dominating two unusual kinds of arenas: networked markets and double-sided markets. And, in both cases, market-share dominance was the key to their success. These two exceptional enterprises exist in singular sectors—lines of business that are very different from the vast majority of markets. Finally, I'll demonstrate how to distinguish between the few industry sectors where market share matters and the majority of cases, where profit alone should sit on the throne.

To be sure, these are definitely special cases. We are venturing into the Bermuda Triangle of business—a place where the usual navigational aids fail and it is easy to lose your way. Microsoft and Visa prospered by learning the bizarre bylaws of their special markets and, even then, each ran into regulatory trouble.

Executives, investors, and regulators often fail to grasp the unique nature of these environments, partly because few sectors truly belong in the exceptional category.

Back in the 1990s, it seemed that every entrepreneur and executive believed he deserved to take the loophole. That's where a lot of crises began. By the end of this chapter, you will know if your company is truly operating in one of the handful of sectors where market share matters most—or whether you're fooling yourself by trying to claim a loophole that isn't rightfully yours. And you will know if you need to address your internal constituencies or admit to them that they may have a point. Either way, you're heading straight for the Twilight Zone of global capitalism.

WHAT ARE NETWORK EFFECTS, ANYWAY?

"Network effects" are what economists sometimes call "network externalities"; that is, "the utility derived from these goods is affected by the number of others using similar or compatible goods," according to Israeli economist Oz Shy's *The Economics of Network Industries,* one of the leading graduate-level economics textbooks in this specialized area.[1]

The most common example of goods affected by "network externalities" is the telephone. No one would buy a phone if there was no one else to call or if there was no reasonable expectation that someone he cared to talk to would soon be getting a phone. This is also true of fax machines, e-mail, cell phones, spreadsheet programs, credit cards, and debit cards, among other things.

This group of users can be called a network. The lack of a network can hamper the development of certain technologies, and businesses that fail to build a network often fail in this type of market.

Consider the fax machine. Early prototypes of the facsimile machine were working in the 1930s. By the 1950s, the makers of fax machines had found a few niche markets, including flight-service stations connected to airports. These stations used the devices to send hourly weather reports to each other—which was a boon to commercial aircraft and flight controllers. But it took almost an hour to transmit one page. For a long time, the technology didn't grow beyond this niche. By the 1970s, there was a faxlike device called a "mojo," which could transmit at the speed of seventeen minutes per page. This enabled early fax makers to capture another market—newspapers that needed the latest reports from foreign correspondents and other "on-location" reporters. In the recent film *Almost Famous,* a *Rolling Stone* writer is told to go to a New York newspaper to use their mojo. When the editor explains how long it takes to send one page, the theater audience chuckles softly. No doubt mojo salesmen got the same response in the early 1970s. Who wanted to fax a 455-page contract to the Chicago office at that speed? It would be faster to fly there with the contract under your arm.

Sometime after 1982, fax machines suddenly began to take off. Why? Fax machine speed had improved considerably—to about three minutes per page. And soon, fax companies were competing on the number of pages per minute.

But fax makers had learned a vital lesson in the 1950s, which helped explain their explosive growth in the 1980s. They focused their sales efforts on outfits that could buy large numbers of machines and create their own internal networks, such as those flight-service stations and newspaper companies. The faster machines opened up the corporate, legal, and medical markets. Each of these segments needed to send large numbers of documents quickly. So the fax makers concentrated on selling batches to companies with scattered offices. For the time being, individual users were ignored. The important race was to create a web of people who needed to exchange information with one another all of the time. And of course these networks could be quickly created through one central purchasing office. Talk about sales efficiency.

The other, related lesson that the fax makers had learned: They needed to create networks of networks, one make of fax needed to be able to send and receive from all the other makes and models. That meant fax makers had to agree on uniform communication standards, which they did. As soon as customers and suppliers realized that they could link up with other corporate communication networks, which might be using another brand or model of fax, they started buying the devices. As the number of users grew, so did demand for faxes. A networked market was born.

By 1987, the majority of American businesses had fax machines—compared with 1981, when almost none did.[2] This is the first example of what computer makers would later call "vertical liftoff," the phenomenon of networks rapidly linking to other networks that touches off an expansion of demand.

ADOBE AND OPEN NETWORKS

The fax machine, built on shared technical standards, is an example of an open network. This is a network where the standards are published and anyone who meets them is free to join.

But not all networks are open. In fact, businesses soon discovered the advantages of owning an open, proprietary network—a network opened to all but owned by one. But it has risks, too.

Adobe, the Santa Clara, California–based software outfit, created one of the first proprietary networks. In the mid-1980s, Adobe's then chief executive, John Warnock, recognized an enormous opportunity. New desktop-publishing programs were flooding the market at the same time that lower-priced laser printers were becoming popular. But the new software had trouble talking to the new hardware. Managers were creating picture perfect reports on screen but were screaming when they couldn't print them out. Or, if they could, the printing house hired to print one million copies of the annual report couldn't open the file. Amid all that corporate anguish, the wailing and gnashing of teeth, a new market was opening, Mr. Warnock realized.

Adobe raced to create PostScript, a standard program for transmitting print-ready documents. Mr. Warnock and his associates went to see the makers of laser printers. Printer manufacturers knew that competition was fierce and that the market was demanding a common standard. Chances are, one manufacturer would get enough market share to define the standard and the smaller fry would either be forced out of business or compelled to retool to emulate the dominant manufacturers de facto standard. Adobe reinforced that message and then asked: "Why go down that road? Why not set a common standard and let the manufacturers compete on price and features, not compatibility?" The benefits were clear: a wide-open market, greater technical certainty for manufacturers and their customers—and a reasonable chance that all of them would still be in business in a year's time.

Meanwhile, other Adobe managers fanned out to meet with software writers. Why undertake all of the costs of writing original code, when PostScript could be incorporated into any word-processing, spreadsheet, or desktop-publishing program? Here Adobe had a head start because its own programs were already testing and using PostScript.

Not every firm signed on at first. But enough did that PostScript became the standard program for computer-printer communication, the *lingua mondo* of printouts.

The more companies that adapted it as their standard, the more others wanted to join the proprietary network. Adobe's standard—its proprietary network—soon became so strong that it survived assaults by mighty Microsoft, then-strong Apple Computer, and others. Today virtually every laser printer, bubble-jet printer, and large-scale publishing outfit in the world uses PostScript.

Again, if Adobe had not secured sufficient market share for PostScript or if enough fax makers had not agreed on a common standard, the attempt to create a network market would have failed. Adobe prospered in a unique market by concentrating like a laser beam on the networking needs of the printer market. A typical profit-centered approach would not have served them as well or at all. They quickly learned the rules of networked markets. Rule number one: Market-share growth is essential. Without critical mass in a networked market, a new product will stall on the runway. With enough initial users, the new product or service will achieve vertical liftoff and become nearly universal.

Case Study: 3DO and Closed Networks

Indeed, that's why 3DO failed to knock Sony PlayStation from its perch. The video-game market isn't linked into a network by technology. Instead, interlocking groups of friends, relatives, and others are the network—and technology either succeeds or fails based on its ability to capture their attention. Most users want to own and play the games their friends play, and few people have enough friends to support multiple video-game platforms. They tend to herd around what they call the "coolest technology." When everyone they know has a PlayStation, that is the game system they will use. This is the market 3DO tried to enter.

In the mid-1990s, 3DO unveiled a new video-game technology and new player, built by Matsushita, which offered lightning-fast play, more realistic graphics, and a daring business plan to topple Sony. It should have been a winner. Users and reviewers loved the games and the player, but it fizzled. Why? Matsushita, the Japanese electronics giant, refused to price the players cheaply enough for teenagers and young men, the key markets for new computer games. Priced out of reach, few bought the 3DO player, and its hoped-for cadres of dedicated fans never appeared. These video games are not solitary entertainments; they are either played by an entire peer group or by no one without that group. Without a large enough network of people to play against, few saw the benefit of forking over their hard-earned cash.

Matsushita's strategy of making a substantial profit on each player would work brilliantly in a nonnetworked market. But in networked markets, market share matters—and the Japanese giant wasn't willing to lose enough to grow share. Without a critical mass of players, user networks never developed. So the effort failed. Matsushita failed to learn rule number two of networked markets: If you make entry prices too high (for a game player or anything else), few will join your network. And if no one joins, your product fails.

THE MYTH OF "LOCK-IN"

Some look at the 3DO example (and others) and say that once a firm dominates a networked market, it cannot be displaced. Some economists call this "lock-in." Unfortunately for big competitors—and fortunately for the rest of us—"lock-in" is nonsense.

Nintendo knocked Atari out of the video-game market and was in turn displaced by Sony PlayStation. Excel's spreadsheet program replaced Lotus 1-2-3. Windows replaced DOS, which replaced CP/M in the operating system market. IBM's personal computers pushed aside the then-dominant Apple II, which had flattened the Altair and the Commodore. Or consider the word-processing market. Wang was the dominant player in the late 1970s, WordStar was top of the heap in the early to mid 1980s, WordPerfect looked like it had ruled the market in the late 1980s, and Microsoft Word has held sway since roughly 1993. At each stage, lock-in enthusiasts would say that the then-dominant firm was set to be the next Standard Oil for a generation or two. And, each time, they were wrong.

THE STRATEGY FOR WINNING IN NETWORK MARKETS

That is not to say that defeating a dominant player is easy. Far from it. One of the things that make networked markets unique is that *incremental improvements are not enough.* To persuade a global network of video-game players or word-processing writers to switch to a new system requires drastic innovation. The improvement has to be *so large* and the benefits *so clear* that large numbers of users are willing to move in a relatively short amount of time. Why does time matter? Because in networked markets, a trickle of new users soon melts back to the old standard if other users in their peer group don't also make the switch. It's not worth the trouble unless others are right behind you. A small trickle over a long period of time probably won't wash away the dominant standard, because the first droplets have already evaporated by the time the second droplets arrive.

So an improved "look and feel" or a few snazzy extra

features usually won't do it. Excel beat Lotus because it could query standard databases and populate the spreadsheet automatically. That saved number crunchers a lot of keyboard time and eliminated transcription errors, which made switching programs worth the bother. And Excel also worked hard at addressing compatibility problems and accessing legacy files. That meant that companies wouldn't have to hire someone to type in all of the old files. That made switching a no-brainer. Lotus did not know what hit them—and survived only because it had another great product in its hip pocket, Lotus Notes.

THE RULE OF SERIAL MONOPOLY

In nonnetworked markets, innovation is incremental and slow; competition is for the customer. In networked markets, innovation is drastic and rapid; competition is for the market itself.

That is why the story of networked markets is one of "serial monopoly." Firms vault to a seemingly dominant position thanks to a pathbreaking product that rapidly wins a large share of the market—and are toppled by unseen competitors with an even better product or service, a few years later.

This kind of volatility is probably unavoidable in networked markets. There can only be one dominant standard at any given time, and there must be a standard to ensure that everyone in the network can exchange files or phone calls or games or whatever with everyone else.

Networked markets are "winner take most." And the nature of networked markets makes them both very risky and very rewarding. The costs of developing a dramatically superior technology and corralling a large number of users is huge. If a rival is better or faster or is just plain luckier, those costs cannot be recouped. You lose. On the other hand, the winning firm enjoys tremendous returns—until it is displaced.

So what can dominant players do to protect their market share—and their futures? Most try to innovate like crazy. As Intel's former CEO Andy Grove put it: "Only the paranoid survive."

This produces a lot of incremental innovation. Sometimes this works. A Microsoft executive told me that adding the "send to" function to Microsoft Word, which enables users to e-mail a document without having to cut, paste, and reformat it—probably helped the product survive for one more product cycle. That's about eighteen months. But I asked what happens when some outfit designs a good e-mail program, with all the benefits of Word? He looked down at his dinner. It was too painful to contemplate. Or imagine if America Online mailed out such a robust e-mail word-processing program to its thirty million global users? Silence. These are the things that keep Microsoft executives awake at night. Remember rule number three: All network monopolies are temporary. Every network market executive has to think like a movie studio executive and ask: What's going to be next year's hit?

AOL AND THE STRATEGIC VALUE OF SWITCHING COSTS

Another strategy for preserving a dominant share in a networked market is to raise the switching costs. Since the actual, monetary costs of switching, say, word-processing programs, is small, the switching costs are measured in trouble and time.

America Online keeps its large installed base of users by getting customers to deposit a part of their personal lives on the network: their online address books. Who wants to retype those? Next, AOL added instant messaging—who wants to miss out on that? Add to that, all those convenient "channels" of proprietary information available on AOL—can you live without those? Yes, you can—but it probably is worth an extra $10 per month to keep them from popping up on your screen.

Rapid imitation of competing benefits and features is another strategy. Other portals have tried giving users free Web pages, free e-mail, and other member-created content. AOL quickly copied these benefits.

DOUBLE-SIDED MARKETS

So far, we have been talking about single-sided networked markets—one company or companies linked to a set of consumers.

There is another breed of networked markets: double-sided markets. In these markets, companies must succeed in winning large market shares in two different markets simultaneously.

Consider Visa and MasterCard. To succeed, Visa needs a large number of consumers to carry their plastic cards and a large number of merchants to accept them. If one set of customers shrinks, the other will gravitate away to other cards. Who wants to carry a card that few stores accept or accept a card that few people carry? And the network effects are powerful. As the number of merchants who accept the card increases, so does the number of people who will want it, and vice versa.

Entering a double-sided market involves a kind of "chicken and egg" problem. An entrepreneur needs sufficient share in two markets simultaneously and he cannot get one without the other.

The first modern plastic credit card was created in 1950, by Diner's Club. The company persuaded a number of popular but pricey restaurants in New York City to accept the card and give Diner's Club 7 percent of the gross bill. The pitch? The spending of wealthy patrons would no longer be constrained by the amount of cash in their wallet, but by their desire to enjoy themselves. As for checks, those sometimes bounce. Diner's Club would take the risk that cardholders wouldn't pay their bills. Once they had talked enough restaurateurs into accepting the card, Diner's Club mailed out cards to well-heeled New Yorkers.

At first, the cards were free. Diner's Club wisely realized that if the first cardholders had to pay extra for the convenience, then they wouldn't use their cards and the whole venture would fail. It worked and soon Diner's Club's success attracted the attention of executives at American Express, which specialized in traveler's checks at the time. Amex entered the market a few years later. American Express had a large base of customers to offer the cards to—but to win merchants it needed to offer a lower fee than Diner's Club. So they initially charged only 5 percent.

By the mid-1960s, the plastic credit card became so lucrative that banks wanted to enter the business. But the barriers looked insurmountable. Few banks had a large market share in any city, let alone nationally or globally. And even fewer had links to potential acceptors of credit

cards—the major retailers. Add to that the costs of admin-
istering a credit card system, building a brand name, and
fighting the two established players. It looked impossible.

Drastic innovation was needed to succeed in this challenging double-sided market. In response, banks formed
a cooperative association to offer Visa cards, which is now
the largest cooperative of any kind in the developed
world. Visa and MasterCard accounted for some $1.6 tril-
lion in charges worldwide in 1999.

The Visa Association remains unusual in the finan-
cial-service sector, but it proved an innovative way to
crack a double-sided market. Some banks specialized in
signing up cardholders (they are known in the trade as
"issuers"), while other banks in the Visa Association specialized in signing up merchants (they are called "acquirers"). In effect, Visa split the double-sided market down
the middle.

The association itself coordinates the two halves of the
double-sided market and coordinates advertising and marketing to strengthen the brand. The association has only a
few levers to control their global network of more than
20,000 banks in more than 200 countries and territories.

- Strict rules of membership. These include "universal
  acceptance," which requires merchants to treat all Visa
  cards alike—and not favor the ones with lower fees or
  charge a surcharge on disfavored cards. Both types of
  banks agree to abide by these rules, and offenders can
  be exiled from the association, a rare event.

- The "interchange fee." Visa and MasterCard charge
  both cardholders and merchants fees for using the Visa
  and MasterCard networks. (So do all other plastic

credit card companies.) The total interchange fee is equal to roughly 2 percent of each charge, but the amount paid by the merchant or the cardholder varies over time. By shifting the bulk of the intercharge fee back and forth between cardholders and vendors, the association can keep the two separate markets in balance. Sometimes the system needs more merchants, so the bulk of fees is shifted to cardholders. At other times, Visa needs more cardholders and the merchants pay most of the fee. "Those selling to a two-sided market must make sure they set prices to attract the optimal mix of buyers on both sides," David S. Evans, a senior vice president at the National Economic Research Associates, told me. Mr. Evans is a consultant, whose clients include Visa.

- Competition among members. Issuing banks and acquiring banks are free to compete against each other and do so vigorously. Some offer lower fees, others frequent-flyer miles. The association keeps the price competition between broad bands, so that the number of users and merchants remains in balance—while allowing banks to compete with one another.

The Visa Association approach has been tried in a number of double-sided markets, everything from long-distance telephony (between customers and providers) through special "dial-around" numbers to online services like Prodigy.

The World Wide Web should allow more firms to enter double-sided markets. Consider ACI, a company that sells software that links to newspapers and advertising agencies. With the ACI service, ad agencies can transmit ads directly to newspapers, and both companies can monitor the frequency of publication and the payment process related to the ads. No longer are ads lost in the mail or payments delayed as New York ad firms try to determine how many times the ad ran in, say, the *Forth Worth Star-Telegram*. Before the Internet, advertising firms were reluctant to buy the service until enough newspapers installed the software to make it worth their while. The newspapers didn't want to invest in the service until they saw the potential to earn ad revenue through it. A classic double-sided market impasse.

When ACI moved to the Web, it was able to quickly acquire market share among newspapers and ad firms. Since every newspaper had Web access, the advertising folks knew they could easily download the program and run the ads. And, because there was the prospect of immediate revenue, the newspapers quickly signed up. "The Web solved the chicken-and-egg problem," notes author Patricia Seybold.[3]

THE BOUNDARIES OF THE EXCEPTIONS

Back in the Internet boom days, every entrepreneur was sure that he was in a networked market where market-share growth was essential.

Part of the problem might have been terminology: "network effects," "networked markets," and so on. A lot of the Web heads, Internet gurus, eager investors, and starry-eyed analysts figured that since users accessed e-commerce sites through some computer network that these were necessarily networked markets. Hardly.

A lot of those Web outfits were not really in networked markets. A user of the now-defunct Pets.com does not directly benefit if his neighbor also buys dog food on Pets.com.

The point about networked markets, too often missed, is that the benefit accrues to *consumers* from adding more users—not to the firm. Every company benefits from more customers.

Networked markets create increasing returns as the number of users increases. In other words, your e-mail becomes more valuable to you as the number of people *within your circle* with e-mail grows. A Chicago lawyer doesn't care how many e-traders in Zanzibar can now read his e-mail. Simply adding users doesn't necessarily increase functionality.

ARE YOU IN A NETWORKED MARKET?

How do you know if your firm is actually in a networked market? Ask some key strategic questions.

- Almost all networked markets are in some form or other in a communication business. Visa communicates between a cardholder and a merchant. ACI transmits ads. Microsoft's Windows allows users to share files. Does your firm enable users to share information with other users—or just between users and the firm? (Hint: eBay is in a networked market and travelocity.com is not.)

- Does that communication add value to users? In the lives of busy people, that amounts to a value proposition.

- If 20 percent of your market share walked away tomorrow, would you still have a viable business? Genuine networked businesses derive a good deal of their value by being the standard mode of communicating something valuable. If too many users migrate to another service, the business suddenly becomes as successful as, say, Diner's Club or Prodigy.

If you are in an actual networked market, remember that your competition is only one innovation away from making you into a dinosaur. Enjoy dominance while you can and stay paranoid.

If you are in a nonnetworked market, welcome to the majority. Now it's time to put market share aside and become a profit leader. In the next chapter, we'll see how to turn any business into a profit leader.

CHAPTER SEVEN

The Rules of Profit Leadership: Why Managers Have to Choose

TOO OFTEN WE MEASURE EVERYTHING AND UNDER-
STAND NOTHING. THE THREE MOST IMPORTANT
THINGS YOU NEED TO MEASURE IN A BUSINESS ARE
CUSTOMER SATISFACTION, EMPLOYEE SATISFACTION,
AND CASH FLOW. IF YOU'RE GROWING CUSTOMER
SATISFACTION, YOUR GLOBAL MARKET SHARE IS
SURE TO GROW, TOO. EMPLOYEE SATISFACTION GETS
YOU PRODUCTIVITY, QUALITY, PRIDE, AND CREATIV-
ITY. AND CASH FLOW IS THE PULSE—THE KEY VITAL
SIGN OF A COMPANY.[1]

—JACK WELCH

Whether we recognize it or not, the world of commerce has essentially two competing philosophies: a market leader philosophy and a profit leader philosophy. And management must choose between these rival schools of thought—managers must either "manage their size" through a market-share strategy or zoom in on profitable growth.

These different philosophies produce different results. Market leaders are large and aim to stay that way. As we saw in Chapter Three, they are captured by their internal constituencies—the executives of large industrial divisions, the unions who work there, the sales force—and their external constituencies—the analysts who focus on share, the press who do the same, the purchasing agents who think big is always best, or at least safer.

Behind these constituencies stand the professors, the gurus, the consultants, and regulators. They have long maintained that larger market shares give companies above-average returns and no amount of evidence will drive them from this dogmatic belief. They see what they want to see. They simply ignore that the market-share theory wasn't designed to be a guide to enhanced profitability, but a rationale for antitrust enforcements and an excuse for being suspicious of big enterprise. As for the insight that *market share alone fails to deliver shareholder value,* they shrug.

They have excuses, evasions, and extenuating circumstances. Nothing can shake the faith of a true believer. As Donald Potter, who runs Windermere Associates and conducted one of the most thorough investigations into the link between market share and profits, told us in Chapter One: "It is like trying to change someone's religion."

Then there is the philosophy of the profit leaders. They have internal and external constituencies, too, but they focus on the needs of an overlooked but essential group: investors. They know the dangers of thinking about size for its own sake or becoming mesmerized by the competition, as we observed in Chapter Four. They arrange their internal incentives—everything from stock options and bonuses to promotions and corporate culture—to drive the company toward shareholder value, as we saw in Chapter Five. It isn't easy and it isn't fast, but it works. And they know something else: Profit becomes more important after the euphoria of a stock-market boom wears off or when the global economy slows. If you are not now managing a profit leader, you need to understand them more than ever—they are your toughest competitors.

The profit leaders know some important things about market share, and therefore about the new rules of competition.

What the profit leader knows can be distilled into two statements: A market-share strategy leads companies to set their sights on the past, not the future; and market share is about the competition, not customers.

Let's unpack these two bundles.

PAST VERSUS FUTURE

Market share is about the past, in every sense. It is calculated by examining and tabulating sales that have already occurred. And, because it is about the past, it is static and lifeless. Look at what is *not* captured by these numbers: *the future potential of some current customers.* We saw how Dell and Roche Diagnostics Systems unlocked the potential of their best customers in Chapter Five.

That's why market-share thinking leads into so many of the pitfalls we saw in Chapter Four. It is a snapshot of the recent past that lulls managers into asking: How do we get more of the same?

And market share is about past competitors and therefore hides future competitors—new entrants who can topple a "dominant" firm and seize a market.

Lego, the Danish toy company, measured itself
against what it thought were its current competitors. And
what they saw looked good to them. The firm held 72 percent of the worldwide construction-toy market in 1995.[2]
Europe looked even better to Lego—it held more than 90
percent of the construction-toy market on the Continent.
Why worry?

Then, Lego executives began noticing that market
share was too narrow a measure of their competition. In
reality, Lego was competing for a share of a child's time,
and children were increasingly playing with video games
and watching television. If Lego wasn't careful, its central
market would move away from them. So the toy maker
began diversifying into electronic toys, even though it
meant expanding the definition of their market and therefore lowering their existing market share. By abandoning
the security of old market definitions, Lego discovered its
true competitors—and reorganized to meet them.

The late CEO of Coca-Cola, Roberto Goizueta,
pushed his executives to define their market as not car-
bonated beverages but all beverages, including water.[3]
This reconfiguration dropped its global market share to 3
percent from 40 percent. But its profits rose by recogniz-
ing the size of the potential before the company—and the
scale of the work it had to do.

Don't confuse a market-share strategy with a growth
strategy. GE does not make this mistake. As Jack Welch
recounts in his letter to shareholders in the 2000 GE
annual report, GE's much-vaunted "Be number one or
number two in a market" strategy was undermined by

internal constituencies. Managers began to "define their markets more and more narrowly to assure that their business would fit the one-or-two share definition." What did Jack Welch do? He told his executives to define their markets so they would have 10 percent or less market share. "Rather than the increasingly limited market opportunity that had come from this number-one or number-two definition that had once served us so well, we now had our eyes widened to the vast opportunity that lay ahead of our product and our service offerings. This simple but very big change, this punch in the nose, and our willingness to see it as the 'better idea,' was a major factor in our acceleration to double-digit-revenue growth rates in the latter half of the '90s," Mr. Welch writes.[4]

Or consider IBM. For more than a decade after the launch of the personal computer, it thought of itself as competing against other PC makers and producers of corporate mainframes. It was single-minded about increasing its share of these markets. And, slowly, Big Blue began paddling toward the rocks. Enter Louis Gerstner. When he became CEO, he quickly recognized something that had eluded all of those market-share mavens. The company had a real expertise in integrating corporate computer systems—a much more profitable business that was then captured by a bunch of firms, including Andersen Consulting, that were not even on the charts back in Armonk, New York. IBM's comeback was built, in large measure, on its strong push into services. "Today IBM earns more money value-added on services than from its hardware, software or middle ware," writes Sandra Vandermerwe.[5] But IBM's opportunities and its competitors would have remained hidden if Mr. Gerstner hadn't looked up from the market-share spreadsheets.

Profit leaders look for *hidden* competitors. Southwest Airlines knows that cars compete with planes on short routes. That's why they make sure that it's cheaper to fly Southwest than to drive yourself. Maybe cars or their equivalent are not part of your market-share definition, but they are part of most customers' choices. In 1980, GE derived 80 percent of its revenues from product sales. By 2000, 70 percent of its revenues came from the sale of services. If it had focused on pushing more and more product sales to increase and retain market share in its existing businesses, it would have been too busy playing the market-share game to expand its market *potential.*

Canon did this brilliantly in the office copier market. Xerox sold expensive machines to corporations that could produce 1,000 copies per minute. But what if a secretary only needed three copies? She had to walk down the hall and wait on line behind other secretaries who also needed only a few copies. Meanwhile, the boss was wondering where his valued assistant was. Enter Canon, with a small desktop copier. Sure, it was slower and cheaper. But it liberated office workers from lines and kept the boss from wondering if they were goldbricking. Canon seized a market that was invisible to the market-share mavens—until it was created.

Another common problem with market-share analysis is that it assumes that the near future will look like the recent past. While this often is a safe assumption, it can lead to some woolly thinking.

Consider the market for microwave ovens in the mid-1990s. Managers and marketers were eager to steal a few share points from their rivals in this highly competitive market. So they benchmarked each other; they assumed that if their product had the features of a competitor's that they would capture the same market share as that competitor. It seemed like a foolproof strategy. At worst, their competitors would have no differentiating advantage and things would get no worse. At best, they would hit on the winning feature and steal a few points. The problem? The market was changing in ways that market-share analysis didn't reveal. Lower-income customers were entering the market and finding all of the new features confusing and costly. Samsung, the Korean appliance maker, quickly seized the opportunity by developing a simple low-priced model. Samsung saw the future and prepared. It couldn't do many of the complex procedures that the higher-priced models (like cooking a rack of lamb) could, but it was good at heating up coffee and soup—what most people use a microwave for.

COMPETITORS VERSUS CUSTOMERS

Market-share data tells managers how they are doing compared with what they perceive their direct competitors are doing.

But what about the customer, who makes every business go?

Market share does not tell us much about customers' satisfaction, beyond the fact that they bought a particular product. But, as we've seen in Chapter Five, delighted customers buy six times more products and services than simply satisfied ones.

That's why Ingram Micro chief executive Jerre Stead is so fixated on customer satisfaction. "What's the most important metric that I track? Customer delight."[6]

By focusing on customer delight, Ingram is strength-ening its potential for *future* business. This takes a lot of work.

"We ask our customers 60 survey questions. I have those questions memorized. They're that important to me. They explore a range of issues—from 'My salesperson thinks of me as a partner and provides me with the tech-nical support I need' to 'When I call Ingram Micro, the phone is answered within three seconds.' Part of our employees' incentive program is based on how customers respond to those questions."[7] Mr. Stead also tracks cus-tomer delight by answering hundreds of e-mails and voice mails every week.

Once companies lift the blinder of market share, new horizons appear. Opportunities beckon. The past passes and the future opens. Competitors fade and customers step into the spotlight. And most important, profit is once again primary—unveiling an objective metric for measur-ing business decisions and assessing leaders' abilities to overcome internal and external constituencies and create shareholder value.

It is time for you to choose: market leadership or profit leadership?

Notes

Chapter One

1. Paul Muolo, "Economies of Scale Are Questioned," *US Banker,* Dec. 6, 2000, p. 78.

2. Harold Demsetz, "Two Systems of Belief About Monopoly," in *Industrial Concentration: The New Learning,* eds. Harvey J. Goldschmid, H. Michael Mann, and J. Fred Weston (Boston: Little, Brown, and Company, 1974), p. 168.

3. Dimitris Bourantas and Yiorgos Mandes, "Does Market Share Lead to Profitability?" *Long Range Planning* 20 (October 1987): 102–108.

4. Robert Jacobson, "Distinguishing Among Theories of the Market Share Effect," *Journal of Marketing* 52 (October 1988): 68–80.

5. Nanette Byrnes and Michael Arndt, "John Dillon's High-Risk Paper Chase," *BusinessWeek* (January 22, 2001): 58.

Chapter Two

1. *Business 2.0,* April 2000.

2. Joe S. Bain, "Relation of Profit Rate to Industry Concentration:

American Manufacturing, 1936–1940," *Quarterly Journal of Economics* 65 (August 1951).

3. Robert D. Buzzell et al., "Market Share: A Key to Profitability," *Harvard Business Review* (January 1975): 97–106.

4. Ibid.

5. Ibid.

6. Ibid.

7. Ibid.

8. GE Annual Report 2000.

9. Ibid.

10. Ibid.

11. Chris Stetkiewicz, "USA: Jetliner Downdraft Clouds Boeing, Airbus Skies," Reuters English News Service, July 15, 2001.

12. Kyung M. Song, "Boeing Sticks to New Business Approach Despite Airbus Claims," *The Seattle Times-Washington,* June 25, 2001.

13. Stetkiewicz, "USA: Jetliner Downdraft."

Chapter Three

1. Donald J. Boudreaux and Burton W. Folson, "Microsoft and Standard Oil: Radical Lessons in Antitrust Reform," *Antitrust Bulletin* 44, no. 3 (Sept. 22, 1999).

2. Ibid.

3. Ibid.

4. Ibid.

Chapter Four

1. John Nathan, *Sony: The Private Life* (New York: HarperCollins Business, 1999), p. 52. This is an excellent book by a writer who deeply understands Japan.

2. Ibid., p. 54.

3. Ibid.

4. Dennis Carey, "A CEO Roundtable on Making Mergers Succeed," *Harvard Business Review,* May 1, 2000, p. 145.

5. Ibid.

6. Jack Trout, *Big Brands, Big Trouble: Lessons Learned the Hard Way* (New York: John Wiley & Sons, 2001), p. 110.

Chapter Five

1. Timothy L. Keiningham, Melinda K. M. Goddard, Terry G. Vavra, and Andrew J. Iaci, "Customer Delight and the Bottom Line," *Marketing Management,* Fall 1999. This excellent article is the basis for much of the Roche Diagnostics case study.

2. Ibid.

3. Ibid.

4. Ibid.

5. Ibid.

6. Ibid.

7. Jay Palmer, "Servers with a Smile," *Barron's* (European edition), June 25, 2001, p. 26.

8. Gary McWilliams, "Dell Fine Tunes Its PC Pricing," *The Wall Street Journal,* June 8, 2001.

9. Ibid.

10. Ibid.

11. Adam Aston, "How Dell Keeps from Stumbling," *BusinessWeek* (European edition), June 18, 2001, p. 4EU6.

12. Ibid., p. 4EU7.

13. Ibid.

14. Palmer, "Servers with a Smile," p. 26.

15. Aston, "How Dell Keeps from Stumbling," p. 4EU6.

16. "Renegade Ryanair," *BusinessWeek*, May 14, 2001, p. 38.

17. Dan Michaels, "Ryanair's CEO Lets Fly," *Wall Street Journal Europe*, March 27, 2001, p. 23.

18. Dan Michaels, "Ryanair Soars on Low Cost," *Wall Street Journal Europe*, Sept. 4, 2000.

19. Michaels, "Ryanair's CEO Lets Fly."

20. Michaels, "Ryanair Soars on Low Cost," p. 29.

21. As calculated by Raymond Jones & Associates's equity research report dated June 9, 2000.

22. Analyst report dated Feb. 15, 2001.

Chapter Six

1. Oz Shy, *The Economics of Network Industries* (Cambridge: Cambridge University Press, 2001).

2. Ibid., p. 3.

3. Patricia Seybold, "Ubiquity Breeds Wealth," *Business 2.0*, Dec. 1, 1998.

Chapter Seven

1. Noel Tichy and Stratford Sherman, *Control Your Destiny or Someone Else Will* (New York: Doubleday Currency, 1993), pp. 240–251.

2. Sandra Vandermerwe, "How Increasing Value to Customers Improves Business Results," *Sloan Management Review*, October 1, 2000.

3. Ram Charan, "The Century's Smartest Bosses Have Influence Beyond Their Companies," *Time*, Dec. 7, 1988.

4. GE 2000 Annual Report, p. 7.

5. Vandermerwe, "How Increasing Value to Customers Improves Business Results."

6. Lucy McCauley, "How Do You Measure Success?" *Financial Post,* May 8, 1999.

7. Ibid.

Acknowledgments

Many people contributed in various ways to the writing and making of this book. Foremost among everyone who helped with this book was Teresa Hartnett, an invaluable agent, sounding board, and friend.

I'd also like to thank my former boss at the *Wall Street Journal Europe,* Therese Raphael, who let me write this book, and George Melloan, who sent me to Europe. Also I'd like to thank some of my former colleagues at the *Wall Street Journal* editorial page whose timely words sent me in new directions: Paul Gigot, Collin Levey, Brendan Miniter, Kim Strassel, and James Taranto.

I'd also like to thank some friends from the corporate world: Daniel Casse, David Evans, and particularly Catherine Windels. Also Stephen Grey at the *Sunday Times* of London.

Ken and Carol Adelman have been a constant source of encouragement and advice. Hats off to Bill Schulz, the late Kenneth Smith, Tony Snow, Michael Barone, Mark Lazenby, Sam Dealey, Horace Cooper, Kevin Washington, Gawain Towler, Tim Beyer Helm, Stuart and Maria Botwright, Henri Lepage, Frits Bolkestein, Joshua Livestro, Gene Karpowski, Cecilia Kundstrand, Hardy Bouillon, and Dr. Tim Evans.

Index

About the Author

RICHARD MINITER has written for the *Wall Street Journal, New York Times, Washington Post,* and the *Sunday Times* of London as well as *Atlantic Monthly, The New Republic,* and *Reader's Digest.* He has appeared on CNN, Fox News Channel, National Public Radio, and other broadcast outlets on both sides of the Atlantic. He has moderated panels of finance ministers at a World Bank conference in Prague and a conference of telecommunications leaders in the European Parliament in Brussels and spoken to audiences of business leaders, journalists, and politicians in America and Europe.

He was formerly an editorial page writer and editor of the *Wall Street Journal Europe*'s Business Europe column.

Currently, he is a senior fellow at the Centre for the New Europe, a leading independent economic-research think tank, in Brussels, Belgium.